AWAITING THE HEALER

To Lois
Christmas 1991
with love from
Maurice, Alison + family

May This book be a
blessing to you Lois -
(I read it first) and as
you turn each page
I've been before you
                love
                Ally
                x x x

To the glory of the Lord Jesus Christ
... and lovingly dedicated to Mother and Dad ...
through whom he has especially expressed his
kindness and love. Through their patient
and understanding hearts, I have drawn much
more than strength.

Awaiting the Healer

MARGIE WILLERS

KINGSWAY PUBLICATIONS
EASTBOURNE

Unless otherwise indicated, biblical quotations are from the
New International Version © 1973, 1978, 1984 by the
International Bible Society.

Cover design by John Billingham

British Library Cataloguing in Publication Data

Willers, Margie
    Awaiting the healer.
    1. Cerebral palsied persons. Biographies
    I. Title
    362.43092

    ISBN 0–86065–924–0

Printed in Great Britain for
KINGSWAY PUBLICATIONS LTD
1 St Anne's Road, Eastbourne, E Sussex BN21 3UN by
Richard Clay Ltd, Bungay, Suffolk
Typset by J&L Composition Ltd, Filey, North Yorkshire

Contents

Acknowledgements

Special thanks to my two co-authors:
Vic Francis is a fine editor from the New Zealand *Challenge Weekly*. Vic's initial working agreement with me was for six months, but writing a book proved a long, gruelling haul ... three years! For his unwavering commitment, patience and stickability, Vic wins my deepest respect and admiration.

Mary Graham is from the pastoral board of the First Presbyterian Church, Papakura and is the unsung hero behind this book. She cared about the 'feel' of the manuscript, and encouraged me to be real, to bring forth the woman God created me to be.

Thanks also to Dianne Mudford and Linda Donald —some of the fastest typing fingers 'down under'; Bill Haythornthwaite—New Zealand book analyst and critic—for his suggestions and helpful advice regarding communicating deep spiritual principles God has weaved into the fabric of my life; and to Pastor Joy Smith, for her faithfulness in prayer and for continually spurring me on to the finishing line.

Foreword

by Jennifer Rees Larcombe

How wonderful that God should give such a great gift of writing to someone who has never used a pen, or create so fine an orator from someone who needed years of speech therapy before she could be understood.

When Margie was born with cerebral palsy doctors told her parents she would never be anything but a vegetable. 'Put her away,' they said. 'Forget you ever had her.' But inside her unco-ordinated, jerky body Margie had a keen brain and a will of iron. Soon she was communicating by pecking at the keys of an electric typewriter by means of a special mouthpiece. What happened next makes compulsive reading.

I first 'met' Margie through the pages of a magazine for disabled Christians, one of the finest of its kind in the world. It speaks for a large organisation for care, support and encouragement and it was Margie herself who first received the vision for its foundation. Her writing helped me profoundly as I struggled to come to terms with my own disability and the burning question of 'why doesn't God heal me?' She helped me to realise (along with countless others who face difficulties of many kinds) that life with handicaps can still be fulfilling and rich. In one issue she wrote, ... let nothing deter you. Great endurance is essential to great achievement.' When you have read this book you will realise just how great have been her achievements and how much endurance they required.

You must be warned that this book is addictive. Not only is it a compelling story, but Margie writes so vividly and with such wisdom I guess you will want to keep coming back to it. This is not just a book for people who have a personal interest in disability, it is a must for everyone. As Margie herself says, 'I believe the word disabled goes far deeper than we at first think. After all, what is 'normal' anyway? What about the warts, wigs, false teeth, broken hearts, broken homes and broken lives?' She also maintains that 'through suffering God teaches us lessons we would not or could not learn any other way. I am convinced that suffering is not to demolish us but to develop us. To know Margie is to realise that what she says is right.

Margie is frequently being told that if only she had more faith she would be healed. I can tell you from experience that it takes infinitely more faith to go on serving and loving God in a wheelchair than ever it takes to walk away from one.

Introduction

This is a book that had to be written. It is the story of a keen Christian, filled with the Holy Spirit, thoroughly convinced that God heals today and that he would heal her. It is the story of the loneliness, confusion and agony when those high expectations of healing were not fulfilled. It is also a story of triumph as God tenderly picks up the broken pieces of a shattered life and fashions a vessel that will bring hope and love to many.

Most people have no problem with divine healing—when healing occurs. It is when healing does not occur that we have our struggles. The temptation to abandon belief in a God who heals arises when, with all the confidence, faith and expectancy that believing Christians can exercise in seeking healing, God remains silent to that request.

How do we minister pastorally to a person whose condition, after prayer for healing, remains or even deteriorates? Is it possible to hold a theology of non-healing at the same time as a theology of healing? What was the response of those not healed at the pool of Bethesda when the man who had lain there for thirty-eight years arose and took up his bed and walked at the healing word of Jesus?

Many things perplex us. Our knowledge is incomplete. We have only a foretaste of the Spirit. Creation is groaning, and so are we, to experience the power of his resurrection and the fellowship of his sufferings. Such biblical statements are, I believe, more applicable to healing than any other topic. The kingdom of God has not yet come in its full power and glory, and many questions remain unanswered. This is not a book recounting the story of an isolated instance of God's grace and power in healing—it is a book recounting the ongoing grace and power of God in the fact of non-healing.

BRIAN HATHAWAY
Pastor
Te Atatu Bible Chapel

Prologue

I staggered to my feet, straining upwards in a desperate attempt to make my lifeless legs respond. As I rose,
my faith welled up within and I waited for God's
healing power to overwhelm my body.

God had brought me 10,000 miles from Auckland to
Los Angeles for a miracle. Here at a service led by
Kathryn Kuhlman, I would for the first time in my life
stand tall. Strength would fill my quivering limbs and
my legs would hold my weight. Now would be the time
when dreaded cerebral palsy would be ousted from my
body, never to return.

For the first time in my life I would walk, run, skip
and dance. I would do up my own buttons, ride a horse
and type with my fingers. I would dial a telephone and
cut up my own food. I would do all those things
'normal' people took for granted.

Now was my time of discovery—that great moment
when I would be normal.

As I strained upwards, certain that God was about to
honour his promise, I was aware of others around me
who were praying too. Their arms were outstretched
towards me and they were believing, with me, for
my healing. Back home in New Zealand there were
hundreds more who were praying and supporting and
believing.

Thousands of prayers had been uttered, and were

being uttered, to a God who cared and loved and healed. The faith of so many was focused in a concentrated and united effort to free my body from the cerebral palsy which had crippled it since birth. I was just one of a mighty Christian army taking part in a supernatural moment—the moment Margie Willers would walk.

As I stretched heavenwards—legs aching from the strain, yet determined to persevere until the healing occurred—I knew my life would never be the same.

'Thank you, Lord, for your healing power,' I breathed. 'Thank you for your love. Thank you for answering my prayers and the prayers of all the others. Thank you for my miracle.'

When the miracle came it was even more dramatic than I had ever dreamed.

Instead of standing firm, pain shot through my tiring legs and I crashed back into my chair. I looked wildly about at a sea of faces and bright lights which were crowding in on my confused and frightened world. I wanted to shout aloud, but somehow I was pinned to my chair, helpless.

And I realised I had been right about only one thing. Life, indeed, would never be the same.

1

Teach Me How to Live

The air was cool and crisp that autumn day; winter was just weeks away. From the kitchen came the smell of coffee and toast, and the clatter of my mother stirring the porridge.

'C'mon, Marg, breakfast,' called my mother down the hall. But lying on my bed in the depths of despair, I did not hear her. I looked down at my legs. From the tops of my knees to my ankles, they were covered in ugly boils. Besides being very disfiguring, they were also unbearably painful, particularly when I left my wheelchair to 'knee-walk' around the house. The boils, resulting from a blood disorder, were the last straw.

I was terribly run down. Cooped up indoors all day, when my spirit wanted to soar and my body wanted to explore, the real Margie was dying deep down inside. Everything seemed stacked against me. Despite working hard I could succeed at nothing. I wondered if life was worth the effort any more.

I'd studied conscientiously and reached University Entrance level at school—a considerable achievement in the circumstances, but to no avail when searching for a job. No one would look at me, considering me too severely disabled, an embarrassment, under-productive. When you are told this often enough, either directly or by inference, you begin to believe it. Eventually, I too considered myself useless and became disheartened.

13

My early spark to achieve my rightful place in society had burned out on the hard hearts of able-bodied people who didn't understand. My life was a physical, mental, emotional and spiritual wreck.

The most obvious deterioration was in my physical condition. My thin body had to work overtime to control awkward and unco-ordinated movements. And I was always susceptible to infections with side effects such as my boils.

Around me a new day was breaking, but wrapped in my cocoon of inward thought I was only vaguely aware of it. Why should I get excited about a new day? Today would be the same as yesterday, and tomorrow would be no better.

'C'mon, Marg, breakfast!'

It was the second or third time my mother had called me. Her words pierced my shell of inward thought, but they didn't make me move. Why should I? I was at the end of my tether. My legs ached abominably, and there was nothing to look forward to—today or any day.

'Marg, *now*,' Mother yelled again, before adding a belated 'please'.

Her insistence finally brought a response from under the bedclothes. I looked across at my wheel-chair, abandoned in the middle of the room, sighed, and heaved myself upright. Straddling my legs over the side of the bed, I fell in an uncontrolled heap on the carpet, then knee-walked to the bathroom—all the time trying to ignore the pain from my lower legs.

As I reached the door, the room began to spin. Nausea swept over me, and the blood drained from my face. I just managed to reach the bath as the whole world closed in around me.

Footsteps scurried to the door and through a fog of pain and wooziness I sensed rather than saw my sister Jennie bending over me.

'I feel ghastly,' I choked. Then, more desperately, 'Get Mum!'

Blackness rushed about me and I lost control. I faintly heard Jennie scream as I hit the floor with a heavy thud.

I lay there, lifeless, unable to move. But the paralysis in my body didn't affect my mind. In fact, my senses were quickened as never before and I felt myself entering a new dimension. A strange but awesome vision opened before me.

I was standing on the bank of a river, its waters gleaming like black onyx. Beyond the dark waters rose a celestial city that appeared to be gold, yet was transparent as glass and beaming with light. I knew instinctively that God was in the city, and I eagerly stretched my arms across the waters towards its beckoning light.

To draw closer, I plunged my foot into the black water. I knew somehow that it was a step towards physical death—and heavenly life. One more step and I would be dead on the bathroom floor, but alive and with God in that wonderful heavenly city. I had no fear of death. Dying would only bring gain—total release from adversity.

My excitement mounted. One more step and it would all be over.

But even as I lifted my other foot to wade into the blackness, I heard the voice of God thundering at me. 'Live!' he commanded. 'There is life ahead of you yet. It is too wonderful to miss. I have chosen you. You are appointed to fulfil an important task. If you do not do it, it will remain undone.'

It would have been easier to die. I didn't want to respond to God's call. I didn't want to live.

Faced with a monumental choice, a battle raged about me. I longed to take the second step towards that celestial city, the city of God. But God had spoken, and spoken clearly. The verdict was life. It had to be. I elected to live.

Without warning the almighty conflict ended. Jennie,

in her second year of nursing training, slapped me hard on the cheek. My faced jerked sideways and she slapped me again.

'C'mon, Marg, breathe,' she insisted. 'Breathe at once!'

'I think she's gone,' Mother muttered in despair.

'No,' Jen interrupted. 'I've found her pulse now. She's coming round. Breathe, Marg, breathe!'

Although it was my decision to choose life, I still resented Jennie's efforts to revive me. Why couldn't she leave me alone and let me die in peace?

She enveloped me in her arms and hoisted me to a sitting position. I gulped a breath, spluttered, and the fogginess began to clear. My body started functioning again.

Mother and Jennie dragged me back to bed and anxiously watched for colour to creep back into my cheeks. I lay there, my breathing still shallow, but my mind clear as I assessed my life anew.

I was in my early twenties, mentally a 'normal' woman, with all the natural feminine desires and emotions. I adored new clothes. I was capable of falling in love. I ate chicken and pavlova.

But I was trapped in a wheelchair. Whether I liked it or not, it was a fact that I would be denied many things in life. I longed to use my academic achievements, but no one would employ me. I began to wonder why I had been educated at all. How in the world could I find a creative outlet, a purpose in life to compensate for the frustration of continually being labelled non-productive?

A great wave of loneliness engulfed me. I had no sense of destiny, no plans, no dreams. 'What's the point of living?' I cried out silently.

And, as he always does in our times of extreme need, God intervened. In the stillness of the morning air, he whispered, 'I do love you, believe me. I have a purpose for your life. You are unique in my plan.'

I turned my head to one side. My Bible lay open on

my bedside cabinet. My eyes suddenly riveted on one particular passage. It was as if the finger of God had enlarged the letters: 'Though [the vision] linger, wait for it; it will certainly come and not delay' (Hab 2:3).

The vision I had just received would not leave my mind. And vision gives hope. I reflected on my early years, the times I'd sensed the call of God on my life, my burning desire to be a missionary. The idea seemed absurd, preposterous, impossible. Yet many times I had closed my door and stayed quietly in my room, reaching for my Bible and turning on a tape of one of my favourite preachers—Leonard Ravenhill, David Wilkerson, Kathryn Kuhlman, Billy Graham. ...And there was no doubt in my mind that the vision of the celestial city had been the call of God.

'Lord,' I cried, 'how can this be real? My speech is so defective, my life so difficult, my faith so limited. If I'm unproductive to man, how can I be productive to you? Why couldn't I have just died and entered that marvellous city?'

God seemed to speak again: 'It is easy to die, but it takes faith to live.'

'Lord,' I prayed, 'I beg you. If you won't let me die, then *you* teach me how to live!'

2

Put Her Away

Imagine an oyster lying on the seabed. One day a grain of sand enters within the oyster's shell. It lies there, causing pain and irritation. Slowly, patiently, and with infinite care, the oyster builds upon the grain of sand —layer upon layer of a white milky substance that covers each sharp corner and coats every cutting edge. And gradually a pearl is made. So the oyster has learned to turn grains of sand into pearls.

I, too, have learned this lesson along my pilgrim way. My name, Margaret, means 'a pearl', and my story is of how God taught me to turn my pain to pearls.

The gates of the New Jerusalem, the Bible tells us, are made of pearl. They are the entrance to the city of God. I have found that every wound in my life has been turned with God's help into a 'pearly gate' through which others have found faith, hope and love. But those gates of pearl have taken years of pain to build as grain after grain of sand has entered my shell.

One such grain entered when I was twelve years old. A hush fell on our noisy classroom as Mr Graffeti looked up from his desk and stared directly at me. Something dramatic was about to happen and my classmates instinctively knew it. The babble of voices died as they waited in anticipation. Graffeti raised his eyebrows, his bushy red moustache twitched as an unpleasant smile slowly curled on his lips. His face slightly forward, he peered over his horn-rimmed glasses and screamed in exasperation. 'Rubbish, just like yourself. Rubbish that nobody knows what to do with.'

By now the class was deathly silent. Silent, that is, apart from my pounding heart and screaming senses as I felt all his derision and frustration focused on me. The incident had started out harmless enough. Graffeti had been recording the results of a class test. My paper had been mistakenly thrown in the rubbish bin, and a classmate had scuttled over to retrieve it for me so that my marks would be recorded.

The 'rubbish' analogy was irrestible to Graffeti, despite the fact that I had answered every question in the test correctly. He looked at me, then at the rubbish bin, and back at me again and pronounced his evaluation of my life's worth for all to hear. Twelve-year-old Margaret Willers was rubbish! For him, the only difference between me and what was in the bin was that there was unfortunately no rubbish tip on which to throw human refuse.

I was born after a three-day labour in January 1948, during which the doctor, it was said, had been more interested in a golf tournament than tending to myself and my mother.

It was a prolonged labour, with many complications. By the time the doctor arrived it was probably already too late. My head was wrongly positioned, caught on the pelvic bone, and lack of oxygen caused what would later be diagnosed as cerebral palsy. Mother and I were fighting for our lives, weakening by the minute, and the delivery team was aware that something was seriously wrong.

Eventually, urgent action was taken. Mother was sedated, I was pushed back and turned into the correct birth position, then delivered with the assistance of forceps.

There was little sign of life. I didn't cry, and I could

only breathe with great difficulty. 'I don't think the
baby will live, do you?' were the last words Mother
heard before she drifted into an exhausted sleep.
Many times during the next few days that pessimistic
prediction almost proved true.

However, Mother possessed a strong fighting spirit.
She was never one to quit. As I hovered between life
and death, she wouldn't give up—and she wasn't
prepared to let her baby do so either.

By the fourth day, despite some close calls, the
report was encouraging. I was crying better, and there
was no fluid on the spine. I would live. Margaret
Willers was alive and almost kicking. Black and blue
from the forceps I may have been, but my dark hair
made me the cutest baby around.

For three months I made slow, painstaking but
steady progress. I was tube fed for the first six weeks as
I had difficulty sucking and swallowing. Once I was
discharged from hospital Mother took on the laborious
task of feeding me. It took nearly two hours for me to
digest one ounce of milk. But she persisted, gently
massaging my cheeks to help me swallow. Through
perseverance and love, I became a chubby, happy and
contented baby—very alert to whatever and whoever
happened to be around.

But at three months the doctor (understandably,
Mother changed doctors after my birth) noticed something amiss. My co-ordination was poor and my movements were out of kilter. Seven months later the fears
were confirmed. A thorough medical examination re-
vealed that I had cerebral palsy of the athetoid type,
the severest degree of disability any child could be
forced to cope with.

It was a shattering experience for my parents to be
told that their child was physically handicapped,
but they had to come to terms with the fact.
Mother listened grimly as the doctor explained what
her daughter Margaret faced in life. I would never be

able to cut up my food. Instead, I would feed myself with a fork or spoon held clumsily in two hands. I would never drink from a glass. Instead I would use a straw. I would never learn to write. The closest thing to walking I would ever achieve would be a kind of crawl-walk on my knees. I would probably never marry or be able to hold down a job, nor would I achieve much of an education. In short, I would never know what it is like to be normal.

Mother suffered greatly from such scathing comments as: 'Didn't you know how to do it properly?', referring to both sexual intercourse and abortion. Such devastating remarks would have destroyed a person of lesser calibre. The medical profession's advice was equally devastating: 'Put her away; institutionalize the child—then forget you ever had her.'

Mother recalls walking through the streets, cradling me tightly in her arms, tears cascading down her cheeks and pleading with her baby—'You will walk, you will learn to read, to write, to run and dance—you will show them, won't you? Prove them wrong!'

My parents investigated every channel of possible help—chiropractors, therapists, masseurs, and a host of different day clinics. It was from The Crippled Children Society that they finally received help and direction. My intelligence was quickly recognised, so it was suggested that the best course of action would be to place me in the new Cerebral Palsy Unit attached to Rotorua's Queen Elizabeth Hospital. This was not an easy decision for my parents to make, for it meant years of separation, but they realised that only there would I receive the necessary treatment and education. I joined the Unit at the age of four-and-a-half. The seven years I was there were ones of sorrow, joy, struggle, humiliation and humour; help from others, and of my own achievement.

I was taught that the handicapped child must fight for her rightful place in the community, and be disciplined in the same way as anyone else. In fact, the programme was one of rigid daily discipline. I applied myself to my physiotherapy and occupational therapy sessions with as much concentrated effort on trying to control and channel the athetosis as anyone could take without going mad. However, it was my speech therapy that was most essential because I was unintelligible to an untrained person. June Opie, author of *Over My Dead Body*, gave me speech instruction for four years. Although she demanded all the co-operation I was capable of giving, she was most understanding and her great sense of humour made speech lessons a source of pleasure.

In 1956 a new headteacher was appointed to the Cerebral Palsy Unit, a man who had been afflicted with polio during his early life. Because of his own handicaps, he understood only too well the battles we would have to face in the future. Each individual child received special interest and understanding from him, for he was determined to enable us to cope adequately with the proceedings of a normal classroom before we were discharged from the Unit. This was by no means easy! At the time I was using large alphabetical stamping blocks to help me write the answers to my lessons. The method was slow, painstaking and messy! However, my teachers discovered that I could hold a big black beauty pencil between my hands and print in large, ugly but quite distinguishable letters.

Then, too, there was the effort of turning the pages of books and the concentration of sitting examinations. During my last year at the Cerebral Palsy Unit I spent one afternoon a week at Rotorua Primary School so I would become acquainted with the environment which I would soon have to face.

Although I never achieved independence in walking, and was discharged from the Unit relying on a self-propelling wheelchair, my parents were determined that my education should not be sacrificed. So at the commencement of the school year in 1959 I attended the Te Puke Primary School. I still used my 'black beauty' pencil, and my exercise 'books' consisted of large sheets of newsprint ruled with lines one to two inches apart, and stapled together. My teacher was most understanding, but to the children I was, at first, nothing but a source of amusement. Despite all sorts of humiliations, however, I was determined to impress upon them that my mental capacity was every bit as good as theirs.

Within a few weeks their attitude changed. Instead of mimicking my defective speech and unco-ordinated movements, they accepted me as an ordinary, intelligent student, showing me their consideration and respect in many ways.

It wasn't until the second year that I was confronted with the man I came to dread—Mr Graffeti.

Graffeti was uneasy in my presence, and his solution to his embarrassment was simple and effective. He banished me from the rest of the class as often as possible, forcing me to work in the isolation of a dismal staffroom. This really frustrated me. I believed that handicapped children should not be segregated. The isolation nullified one of the main reasons I was attending school—interaction with able-bodied people.

However, despite his dismissal of me as a person and his labelling me as 'rubbish' in front of the whole class, Graffeti unintentionally provided me with the tool which revolutionised my life. He introduced me to the typewriter. An old model was acquired—Graffeti was fascinated to see what I could accomplish on such a machine. At first it didn't seem too promising as my fingers were not co-operative or strong enough for striking the keys. Typing involved entire body movement. My mouth would open, I would bash the key, my tongue would do a circuit, the key would noisily clatter, the typewriter would vibrate indignantly, my mouth, dry, would suddenly close and another letter would appear on paper!

My hands were obviously inadequate for the job, so eventually I used a piece of dowelling-wood, holding it in two hands like a pencil and tapping the keys with it. This method immediately began to produce a higher standard of work.

I don't consider I have much for which to thank Mr Graffeti, but for his decision to introduce me to the typewriter I shall be for ever grateful. In May 1960, he was transferred to another school, and was replaced by Brian Dixon.

Brian Dixon was new to the district. He believed in strict discipline and demanded a high standard of work from all who were capable. Our previous teacher had been rather lenient, and as a result we were quite an unruly class. This was something our new teacher was not going to tolerate and within a few days we were changed children.

Brian Dixon took a very special interest in my welfare and development. I responded with deep affection and respect. For a time he found my disability a tremendous battle. He could not understand a word I spoke, but could read my big jerky printing and found I was intelligent. He soon learned to ask me questions that required a 'yes' or a 'no' answer to which I could shake or nod my head appropriately. He was a wonderful man who determined to do all in his power to help me.

Brian wrote later of his early impressions of me:

I will never forget the challenge you placed in my lap when I took over that very unruly class in May 1960. I wondered what I had struck! When I saw you, and your piece of dowelling and your black beauty pencil the only thing which saved me was your captivating smile, your advanced sense of humour and a look in your eye which seemed to say, 'What's he going to do with me?'

I knew how to love you—that was easy because you

were such a bundle of smiling mischief, but I didn't have a clue as to how to help an intelligent child who was having difficulty in expressing her knowledge and personality through the usual forms of communication, writing and speaking. You worried me a great deal and when you mentioned that June Opie had taught you, I wrote to her and simply said, 'I have Margaret. What the dickens should I be doing with her?'

June wrote back:

Margaret had one of the best brains in the Unit, and one of the worst physical handicaps. Her tragedy is that her brain damage has caused severe motor (or purely physical) disturbance, yet left her centres of intelligence absolutely unimpaired. Such cases are rare.

She was always co-operative, quick-witted and surprisingly objective about her handicap, though justifiably 'tiggy' at times. She will face a tremendous upheaval during adolescence, and you can do much to help her through a sticky time by encouraging her in her intellectual and vocational pursuits. She has persevered and achieved wonders—as the mere fact she can sit in a chair denotes. She will probably never walk, but if she wants to, let her try.

June recommended Brian allow me the use of a typewriter at all times.

It will be her only means of reasonable expression and communication. Unless she enjoys the pencils (you are right to use large ones) I would cut them out altogether, giving her freedom with finger painting on large pieces of paper on the floor and assuage her love of colour and movement.

Her speech will always be defective, but it should be intelligible. The trouble begins with lack of co-ordination of her respiratory muscles, and this is aggravated by severe jerky movements of trunk, arms, shoulders and face whenever she wants to speak.

I don't know, if, or how, she is managing to turn pages of a book. If she has solved the problem herself then that is excellent. If not, then you could perhaps adapt something for her. I like these people handling things (particularly books), but this, in Margaret's case, often means death to the thing. She loves reading, as you doubtless know, and the more she can do on her own the better.

She has a pretty rugged time ahead of her. As she matures she will be faced with the fact that she will not have a normal adolescent social life. If she can be doing something useful by then, she will find happiness in feeling useful, and thus necessary. If not, she may throw in the sponge altogether. If you can gear her teaching towards her successful adjustment in the normal stream of life—ie typist in a Public Trust Office, or Social Security Department where she will find friends of her own age, then you will be doing a grand job.

She is a born worker, and will never be happy sitting back drawing Invalid Benefit.

Armed with this information, Brian Dixon created an environment at school in which I thrived. I was never again placed in the disused staffroom to work alone. Instead the typewriter was brought into the classroom and once again I began full classroom participation.

'Do you think I'm rubbish?' I asked Brian suddenly and nervously one day, still wounded from Graffeti's callous remarks over a year earlier.

'You are my bag of jewels, Margaret,' he said. 'Together we will concentrate on your precious gifts and qualities—we will make them shine.'

In retrospect, I realise there was only one basic difference between Brian Dixon and Mr Graffeti. Neither had encountered anyone like me before. One rose to the challenge, the other copped out.

As a student, I discovered the best therapy for any disabled person is the challenge of competing with the able-bodied. When you are continually with other handicapped children you can grunt and groan together. You understand each other. But this is totally unacceptable in an able-bodied environment. In the real world people do not make allowances. They expect you to be and act like them, and if you don't come up to their expectations you will be left behind. This inflicts great pressure upon the disabled person, but it is a marvellous way of lifting you above your circumstances.

My greatest discovery back in those school days came from June Opie's suggestion to Brian Dixon that an electric typewriter would cause less physical exhaustion than a manual machine. My parents could not afford to provide one, so Brian took up the cause, reminding me of the little turtle—'You don't get anywhere unless you stick your neck out.' He sure did stick his neck out for me!

Eventually, the headmaster of the Te Puke Primary School approached the local Rotary Club and a cheque for $120 NZ was written out that night! The Tauranga Branch of the NZ Crippled Children Society sent their field officer to ask my teacher if I could in fact use such a machine. Finding that I could, she reported back to the Society and another cheque for $100 NZ arrived.

Finally, a typewriter salesman said his firm would reduce the price if the Education Board agreed to a dollar-for-dollar subsidy. I will never forget the delight and excitement as one of the boys rose on my behalf and beautifully expressed my gratitude. 'I'm sure it is going to be very beneficial for Margaret,' he said. 'I'm sure she'll go far with it in the future.'

Prophetic words indeed.

It took a great deal of hard work to become completely proficient on the new machine, but by the middle of the year I'd improved—so much so, that Brian Dixon was eager for me to sit my mid-year examinations without his assistance. I agreed to take the plunge. As we entered the classroom for the exam, an unusual degree of tension filled the air. My classmates were aware of the hurdles I faced. The bell rang. We attacked our two-and-a-half page essays, an hour-long exam. My fingers began to strike the keys of my typewriter, my mind overflowing with words and ideas.

Ten minutes passed. It seemed like an eternity! My arms ached and my head throbbed from the constant effort and concentration. Another twenty minutes. I could feel my brain swimming in a sea of words which made no sense. I began to panic. With just half an hour left, I hadn't even completed half a page. Frustration and exhaustion were beginning to take over. The strain was so great that my whole body grew tense, and perspiration ran down my face as I valiantly tried to finish my paper. I was determined not to fail. I grabbed a pencil and in desperation tried tapping the keys. But the method was too slow.

Suddenly an idea flashed through my mind—*my tongue*. I would type with my tongue. Down went my head. Words became sentences, and sentences became paragraphs. My pitiful half-page grew rapidly as I raced through the rest of the essay.

As the room filled with the continuous clicking of keys—replacing the hesitant typing the class was used to—the other children stopped altogether. They forget their exam as they watched intrigued at the bizarre sight of my head bobbing up and down, my tongue flashing over the keyboard.

The exam finished. I had accomplished my goal. I sat back, exhausted, but I had overcome one more mountain—my way! That afternoon my efforts were rewarded. When the results were announced I had gained the highest mark in the class.

About this time I became aware of the demands my wheelchair imposed on my younger sister, Helen. She was responsible for wheeling me to and from school. By the end of the day I was very tired and preoccupied with getting home. However, at this stage of the day Helen was exhilarated and bursting to join in recreational and after-school activities. On several occasions the frustration and tension was so great that by the time we rolled in through the kitchen door, we were almost ready to kill one another. Recognition of this fact led me to persuade my parents to explore the possibility of obtaining a three-wheel cycle.

Again, they could not afford to buy one, but the Crippled Children Society had an unused, ancient model. I was willing to try anything. If it provided a means of transporting myself to school, and freed me to undertake adventures on my own, it would be worth it.

The three-wheeler, an adult-sized machine, arrived. I was very small to handle such a monster, but we lowered and raised everything possible in order to fit my requirements. New tyres were put on and the pedals were fitted with the boot-fittings from an old pair of skates.

In order for me to stay perched, albeit rather precariously, on the high seat, my feet were strapped and tied to the pedals, and once my hands were secured on the handlebars I had a good grip to hold my balance.

Everything I did on that tricycle was at top speed! What a menace I was on the footpath, though I didn't realise it at the time, as I raced downhill from home to school. Everyone I met—be they small or large, young or old—had to jump for their lives when I approached, out of control and travelling at top speed!

My other problem was that I didn't always manage to apply the brakes properly at the school gates, and this resulted in many encounters with the ground. Let loose like that, it is a miracle nobody was killed! And, amazingly, I have few scars to show for my hare-brained driving. A hedge strategically planted alongside the main gate often acted as a buffer.

My mother was absolutely incredible throughout what was often a very trying ordeal. She never mollycoddled me. Had she done so it would have ruined my life. She was tough talk with a tender heart. Many disabled people believe the world owes them something because of their disability. But Mother never fell into this trap. She treated me just like the rest of the family. If I needed a belting she administered one—and for this I am grateful.

Mother's commitment to me was so much above the call of duty. After me came three other children: Helen, two years my junior, Jennie another four years later, and my brother John two years later still. The amount of time and input she gave to me had to be balanced against the needs of the other three kids and Dad. We were all treated as individuals—that was a real achievement. She was an exceptional mother—accompanying me on school trips, dressing me beautifully despite our financial struggles, and involving me in every way possible in what she was doing. I would sit cross-legged on the floor with a baking bowl squeezed between my legs, a wooden spoon between my two hands, and draped with tea towels as I mixed a cake. With concentrated effort, I would stir the mixture as best I could, and the resulting mess didn't seem to matter. The important issue was that I was being creative (again—my way!)

It is essential to the development of disabled people that we feel, touch and explore. Mother never prevented me from exploring on the pretext that I would get too grubby, or that it was too inconvenient.

And, just as she allowed me the freedom to explore, she encouraged me to make believe, to dream, to extend my mind as far as possible. She could clothe me in a pretty dress, drape a lace table cloth about my head, produce flowers from the garden and I would dream of being a bride or a fairy-tale princess. It was marvellous—something every little girl loves, but unfortunately something that not all disabled children are encouraged to enter into.

Mother's efforts inspired me to rewrite the definition of true love: love is giving *time*. I believe there is truth in the saying that the majority of women are capable of child-bearing, but not all are capable of being real mothers. My mother gave quality time. I

shudder to think where I would be today without
that.

She battled with her own emotional conflicts throughout this time, struggling to find answers to endless
questions. Why was I being educated? What do you do
with a child who is so handicapped? What would my
future be? Would she be forced to look after me for
the rest of her life?

Her efforts remind me of the famous Jew, Victor
Frankl, who was thrown into a concentration camp in
Nazi Germany. When he was brought before the
Gestapo, they stripped him—even demanding his
wedding ring. As he removed the ring, he thought,
'They can take my ring, but there's one thing nobody
can take from me—my freedom to choose how I
respond to what happens to me.'

On the strength of that, he not only survived the
holocaust, but developed the whole psychiatric system
called logotherapy, which states: 'When you find meaning in everything, you can face anything.'

Frankl survived the horrors of the holocaust because
he was sustained by an inner conviction that he would
come through it, and that he would be able to use his
suffering to good effect.

Mother possessed those same qualities and convictions. Through the years, tough as they were, she
worked to cultivate and impart into my life that same
drive and desire to conquer and overcome—and to
respond to difficulties with a positive attitude and
outlook. And that's what happened, not without regular
heartbreak, but it happened.

3
'For Heaven's Sake'

There is truth in the saying 'Even an ordinary horse can be quite outstanding in his or her own field.' A couple of years had lapsed. I was now one of the crowd. I had won several English prizes and was progressing well with my studies.

My secondary education was gained through New Zealand's Correspondence School in Wellington. The local Te Puke High School with its two-storey block was not accessible because of my wheelchair. I found my assignments challenging. The study material was of a high standard, always detailed and excellently illustrated—which compensated for the lack of a personal tutor and a blackboard.

My teachers were well qualified and dedicated, taking a personal interest in my education. They too were optimistic about my future, encouraging me to concentrate on English and explore journalism. They always exorted me to keep my mind active, extend my vocabulary, read widely and write at every possible opportunity. 'You never know,' they'd encourage, 'one day you may even write your own book! Perhaps an autobiography, similar to June Opie's!'

I had my reservations. Write a book! That was a marathon task, well beyond my capabilities. Nevertheless, the challenge lay like a seed deep within me, dormant until recent years. It was during my time with the Correspondence School that a typing fixture was devised, uniquely for me, by an occupational therapist.

This amazing apparatus consisted of a six-inch pointer strapped to my forehead. Through sheer grit, hours of patience and dogged determination I gained mastery of my 'head-wand' and within a very short period mastered sufficient skills to gain my licence on the keyboard. When I opened up throttle, my top speed was about forty words a minute (faster than a two-finger typist!) The idea behind this new invention was to improve the hygiene and presentation of my work—typing with my tongue limited my future employment prospects!

I did not find my studies or homework easy. I often felt exhausted and ill, but I knew I had to persevere in order to achieve some kind of goal. Although I was unable to sit all my major examinations, I received qualifying passes in both English and typing, and also the Chamber of Commerce examinations, with a 75% pass.

During the latter part of my secondary education, my correspondence studies were complemented with tuition from Tauranga Girls' College which was twenty miles from home and the only college nearby which could accommodate my chair. I was overwhelmed with the help I received from staff and students. Nothing was too much trouble. My typing teacher particularly was more than determined that I would receive the same training as the other students, and that I would pass my examination with good marks—even if it meant she moved heaven and earth to help me achieve this.

A wonderful friend helped me in my English classes and willingly wrote my notes when we attended lectures. Manoeuvring my chair from class to class at the end of lessons created little problem for my fellow-students. One girl would wheel me, while another would wheel the trolley which carried my electric typewriter.

At times, however, changes between classes did prove challenging. If for some reason time was running short, we'd often have to dash across campus. My chair, which was not easy to control at anytime, would go into over-drive—over the rose gardens and through whatever obstacle was in its path. Amid the laughter I'd be reinstated on my throne and dusted down, my jellybeans (my supplementary energy source) would be gathered from their scattered resting places, and my books retrieved. And then off we'd race again. These hysterical escapades occurred frequently and I became adept at suppressing my mirth in front of my more serious tutors.

This year was the high point academically, socially and personally. Together with my classmates and tutors I conquered new mountains. I well remember the day I overcame one of my greatest fears—reading aloud in class!

For some weeks the class had been reading its way through Shakespeare's *Twelfth Night*. This particular day I decided to take the plunge and participate in the form's drama activities. My textbook was rather fragile because of its age, and as I squawked and squeaked through my paragraph, my nervous vibrations shook me, the desk, the chair and the book. By the time my marathon twelve-line speech finished my text lay in tatters! I was so petrified that I'd vibrated the pages right out of their spine! It is doubtful whether anyone understood a word of what I read, but as the weeks passed my text suffered less and I became a reasonably coherent play-reader.

I was unsuccessful in gaining my university entrance (failing by only two marks, through insufficient time). For me, this is a mountain which remains unconquered. However, I have several friends with the same disability as myself who are university graduates, so it can be done!

During these years, I learned the key principle that

living can be giving—but it's a two-way process. A person can make a living by what they get, or they can make a life by what they give. My aim was the latter.

Attitudes are so important, I discovered. It is essential to develop and foster positive, creative attitudes, even when bombarded with odds. I could choose to be negative or positive. It just depended on how I looked at situations. I could regret that rose bushes had thorns, or choose to rejoice that thorn bushes had roses!

Up until my teenage years, my father regarded my severe disabilities as thorns—something he struggled to accept. Like many men do when confronted with threatening situations they can't handle, he cut himself off. We'd be in the same room—he'd be there, but not really there. Our relationship tended to be impersonal. Our minds never met nor did our understandings, experiences or personalities touch. Nevertheless, Dad was loyal, helpful and practical. But there was a missing bond, a lack of warmth.

Nothing is ever gained by avoiding reality. The only way to alter our lives is to alter our attitude of mind. And that's what Dad had to do. Finally, my roses of academic achievement brought about a change in his attitude, and in due course he tangibly expressed his appreciation of my efforts and abilities. A rapport developed between us as our respect for one another grew. Dad became more sensitive towards my needs. With dedication and diligence he'd maintain and clean my chair, provide transport, and make our home more accessible to me.

Side by side with my academic growth ran my spiritual growth. I had been brought up in a good Christian environment, and I became a Christian when I was seven years old. It was a simple decision made with the natural innocence and trust of one so young. Yet it was also a deeply profound decision, without a doubt the most life-changing force I would ever experience—one which has enabled me through the rest of my life!

It was in hospital that I actually committed myself to Christ. I'd been unwell for several days and when my condition suddenly worsened I was rushed into hospital with a grumbling appendix. My stay in the ward proved a frightening ordeal. My unintelligible speech meant no one understood my requests for drinks or bed pans. And the sterility of the surroundings only increased my apprehension.

Ultimately, the grumbling appendix didn't result in surgery. However, God used the situation for good. The ward programme included a weekly Bible Hour for children. During this special hour, the truth about Jesus Christ was made crystal clear. The message was simple: 'God so loved the world that he gave his one and only Son, that whoever believes in him shall not perish but have eternal life' (Jn 3:16).

I'd always had a spiritual awareness, but that night I faced a choice. I wasn't a puppet or a robot. I was a free person—free to make my own decisions. I could invite Christ into my life to be my Saviour and be born again, or I could turn my back and reject him!

With rapt attention I listened as the speaker described the life and work of Jesus Christ: his humble birth, his work in the carpenter's shop in Nazareth, healing the sick, performing mighty miracles of raising the dead. And then there was Calvary, the pain, the suffering of the Saviour who entered this world and died in agony on a cross for me. He was buried in a tomb, and he rose in a real body.

When I heard the gospel described like this, I could do nothing but believe it. I realised that without Jesus Christ I was sunk. So I bowed my head and invited Christ into my life.

From that time onwards he has grown to mean everything to me. Like the apostle Paul, I could boast that the gospel is the power of God unto salvation. I was never ashamed of my faith. Immediately my one aim in life was to become a missionary. In those days I probably knew more about the power of prayer than I exercise today. It thrilled me. Mentally I'd wander up and down the streets of my home town, in my mind's eye praying for people in our neighbourhood.

My continual insistence that I was going to be a missionary when I grew up frequently embarrassed my mother who did her utmost to deter me, to have me face reality.

'Marg, don't be ridiculous, it's impossible,' she'd sigh in exasperation. 'You are far too handicapped—the Board for Missions would never accept you!'

I maintained strong spiritual convictions that if the impossible is the only obstacle then it can be done! After all, I reasoned, wasn't it Hudson Taylor, the man who founded the China Inland Mission from which hundreds of missionaries were launched out into service, who once said: 'When God does anything, we find firstly, it is impossible, secondly, it is difficult, and thirdly, it is done!'? God specialises in things termed 'impossible'.

Mother talked until she was blue in the face, but she never succeeded in dampening my enthusiasm, or knocking this 'obsession' out of me.

When I was sixteen to twenty years of age, two incidents in particular had a dramatic impact upon my Christian life. The first was while attending a summer convention where the speaker's message to the young people was on 'Untapped Potential'. Throughout his rousing address he exhorted young people to discover their hidden potential—their God-given abilities—and shake themselves out of apathy and complacency. Everyone was born with creative skills they could develop for the kingdom of God's sake!

The challenge came with great force when the evangelist related a story about a young disabled

woman named Helen McKenzie. Helen was about my
own age and also confined to a wheelchair. Her body
and hands were badly deformed. One day she attended a convention similar to the one I was attending.
At that gathering the speaker also pleaded for young
people to stop hankering after the 'bright lights of
this world' and launch out into greater discoveries
—to reach for the best God had in mind for their
lives.

At the close of this address, young Helen McKenzie
asked to be wheeled up to the altar rail where she could
speak with the evangelist. She was desperate to do
something—absolutely *anything*, for God. But the
question was, what on earth could she do for heaven's
sake?

The evangelist had no answers, but sensing the
young woman's passion to tell others about the salvation that could be theirs in Christ, he bowed in
prayer, simply asking God to grant the desires of her
heart.

Some weeks passed. Then one day as she was reading down the death column of a newspaper, Helen
suddenly became aware of hundreds of people who
were lonely and grieving.

God had answered her cry. What a missionfield
she'd found! With her deformed hands she taught
herself to type and each day she disciplined herself to
write to these bereaved people—communicating the
gospel to them.

For ten years she performed this unique ministry.
Then she died.

After her funeral, friends were invited to visit her
room. Inside they came across two trunks, one labelled
'Sinners'; the other 'Saints'. Intrigued, they opened
them and found to their amazement hundreds of
letters from Catholics, Jews and Protestants—letters
which testified of their having been won to Christ
through her bright testimony.

Helen McKenzie's story shook me to the core. I left that meeting determined to serve the Lord as never before.

The second incident which reinforced my calling included the story of a lady who lived in South America, early this century. At the height of her career she was seized with a dreadful disease, and to save her life doctors first amputated her legs, then her arms, leaving just the trunk of her body.

'Where's a God of love in such tragedy?' we might exclaim. However, there are some things in this life we will never have answers for. In spite of her calamities, this lady did not lose her faith. Her relationship with God was so deep that stepping into her room, one sensed an immediate awareness of his overwhelming presence. It was as if there were angels all around.

People travelled great distances seeking her wise counsel and powerful prayers. These encounters renewed people's zeal and often led them into spiritual warfare for their individuals, churches and nations.

She was a true prayer warrior, and her prayers moved the hands of God in wonderful, mysterious ways. Although her physical condition continued to deteriorate, she was determined not to lie in bed and vegetate. 'It's the spirit that counts—not the body!' she'd affirm, then quote: 'Only one life 'twill soon be past—only what's done for Christ will last!'

A carpenter devised a gadget which fitted around her shoulder blades. From this extended a steel rod with a pen attached to it. To write involved using entire body movements, yet her penmanship was beautiful. Using this unique device, she wrote an amazing number of letters, proclaiming that the love of God is greater by far than man or her pen could ever tell.

Two years later, this remarkable lady was 'promoted to glory'. Her funeral was a service of great triumph.

After the 'celebration service', the pastor visited her room. On the wall above the bed hung a text which read: 'Out of her innermost being shall flow rivers of living water.' Beside the bed, he noticed a large trunk which he opened. To his astonishment, he found 1,500 letters—all replies from people who'd become Christians through her ministry during the past two years.

This was a challenge to myself, but it must have been an even greater challenge to my 'normal' Christian friends—friends who had all their faculties.

I asked myself the question, 'What on earth was I really doing, for heaven's sake?' And I responded to the challenge of these remarkable women by regarding my typewriter as a new driving force to correspond with missionaries in many remote parts of the world and to type letters of encouragement to friends and people whom God brought across my path in various ways.

The Christian life is one of constant challenge. In my pursuit of excellence I applied myself diligently to memorising passages of Scripture. My hunger to learn the word of God became insatiable. It was no great feat to memorise twenty to thirty Bible verses a week— sometimes more! This culminated in my winning several first prize awards during my Bible class years. My Bible class teacher for those four years took time out, sitting with me and listening carefully while I recited large chunks of Scripture. He was a wonderful man, patient, kind and caring—always giving of himself. I well remember tackling the whole of Psalm 119—all 176 verses. It was a marathon effort for both my teacher and myself!

Memorising Bible passages verse by verse also highlighted how the Christian life is a process of growth in which we advance from one stage to the next. From spiritual infancy to maturity, from milk to strong meat, from being rooted in Christ to being firmly established.

We're often eager to be grown up all at once, but we must learn to take a step at a time, day by day year by year.

The next milestone in my life was my twenty-first birthday. My parents were determined this event would be particularly memorable—a replacement for the wedding I was unlikely to have. Nearly 200 people were invited to this celebration.

As I approached my coming of age I wished desperately that I could be miraculously healed in front of all my guests. It would be so exciting to get up out of my chair, and stand tall, with perfect body co-ordination. How we'd all praise God as we saw his wonder and power.

I was alone in my room visualising the scene, when I began to wrestle with questions—questions to which at this stage of my life there were no answers.

'Lord,' I enquired, anxiously, 'will I ever have a career? Will I ever marry? Will I ever experience the joys, the privileges other young women take for granted?' And the question I wrestled with most of all: 'Will I ever leave my chair?'

As a young girl I often longed for a vision. I wished I could see Jesus with my own eyes. How this would encourage my faith and help me through times of difficulty.

Now on the eve of my twenty-first birthday I poured out my heart to the Lord. Questions, fears, frustrations and anxieties tumbled out. And as I shared my inner feelings with him, his presence tangibly entered the room. In the stillness of the night, his figure, dressed in soft flowing garments, stood at the end of my bed.

My fears vanished. It was Jesus! He'd come! That was the most wonderful birthday gift of all. He stood quietly, his presence bringing comfort and security. In a gentle whisper he spoke with me, and answered my questions.

'My child, I understand your concerns. You have not chosen this course, but I have chosen you. Your chair is for a purpose. I cannot take you out. There's no one I can trust but you. Should I heal you now, I have no one to put back in your chair. My plan is mapped out. You must persevere—and press onward with determination, courage, tenacity and resolution. I have no other plan.'

I was young and very immature. But even then I was excited to be a marked person—marked by the Spirit of God.

Sadly, through the years that followed, the memory of Jesus' twenty-first birthday gift—that special calling in God—faded as I fought against his purpose and forged ahead with my own visions, dreams and pursuits.

The following evening I sat in my chair facing my guests, before being wheeled centre stage to deliver my speech, the climax of that memorable birthday party. I had several moments in which to pause and reflect. My mind roamed back through the scenes of the past twenty-one years. Familiar faces came to mind. June Opie, Brian Dixon, my friends, my family—people God had brought into my life to help mould and make me. People who helped develop my personality and character. I praised him for it all—laughter, tears, trials, fun and pain. It had all been part of growing up.

As I turned to the crowd a hush pervaded the building. It was a sacred moment as God came down and tangibly imparted something of himself to the people.

My voice was strong, clear and confident as I testified to God's grace over the years, recounting some of the challenges, frustrations and triumphs, and acknowledging those who had come alongside and helped me thus far. In conclusion, I recounted the vision of the previous evening.

People sat, over-awed, tears trickling down their faces. The majority present loved and accepted me, but until that moment they'd never understood a word I spoke. The sovereignty of God was undeniably demonstrated as my words penetrated their hearts and lives.

'You've never spoken like that before!' one friend cried ecstatically as she threw her arms around my neck. 'Your speech was so clear ... as clear as a bell. That's got to be God—all God!'

'God is a God of wonders and miracles. He could do what no man could. Only he could give me a voice. Truly it was not by might, nor by power, but by his Spirit. I believed this divine encounter was only a foretaste of the best that was yet to come.

I'm aware God doesn't grant special visions to everyone, neither does he intervene in dramatic ways to change their lives. We are all individuals and God deals with us individually. God is a God of variety—each person is uniquely special to him.

Ahead of me now stretched my adult life—new challenges, hurdles, choices, changes—a life of adventure and discovery. As my mind roamed back over those first twenty-one years there was no denying the battle. It had been hard, yet I sensed God weaving his purpose into my life, and steering its direction.

I would like to conclude this section of my life with a simple but delightful story about two frogs. In the dead of night, two lively green frogs were jumping freely around a beautiful garden. They were having the time of their lives. Unknown to them, however, the owners had dined outside that evening and forgotten to clear away a bowl of cream. In their glee, the two frogs accidently jumped, plop, right into the bowl.

The first little fellow, fascinated by the taste, greedily gulped down the mixture. He gulped too much—

and drowned! But the second little chap was determined to escape. Frantically he flip-flopped round and round.

The hours ticked by, and he grew more and more exhausted. His situation appeared utterly hopeless, but he persisted. Somehow he managed to keep himself moving. When morning broke, there he sat—on a pat of butter!

Twenty-one years' experience had convinced me that God does help those who help themselves. Though the odds are against us, we must persevere until we come out on top. Living is a matter of surviving!

I'd also learned that ordinary horses like myself can be quite outstanding in their own field. I felt I could look back on my twenty-one years with some satisfaction of my achievements. Little did I realise, however, that even greater challenges and trauma lay ahead.

4

The Encounter

I have always believed that God would teach me how to live. Not just to exist, but to live life to the full.

I enjoyed a whirl of activities—young people's camps, Bible class, opera and various musical productions. I loved music! However, my great frustration in life was the lack of a career—an unfulfilled desire to enter the work force.

My family strove hard to whet my appetite for creativity. People helped to fill the gap. Outside the family, friends broadened my horizons by inviting me into their homes.

My second home was that of one of New Zealand's foremost sheep shearers, world champion Ivan Bowen and his wife Joyce. Uncle Ivan and Aunty Joyce (as I called them) were like my second parents and their daughter, Kathy, was my closest friend.

The Bowens ran an open house—more like a railway station than what most people would consider home. Their home was fascinating, reflecting their rural lifestyle—large rambling rooms full of stuffed ducks flying from the ceiling, deer heads complete with magnificent antlers, stuffed pheasants on stands and deer hides strewn over couches. One had to be a dab hand at wheeling a chair through cluttered corridors, so as not to collide with one of Uncle Ivan's prized trophies, or mow down one of Aunty Joyce's pot plants. It certainly was a family home—lots of activity, colour and always the smell of baking pervading the rooms.

The Bowens were deeply committed Christians. Uncle Ivan was often away from home on preaching engagements, while people from all walks of life and from every denomination either visited or stayed at their homestead. During mealtimes, I often sat spellbound, intrigued by the flow of stimulating conversation.

During one of my visits something happened which shattered every notion I ever had about the power of God to heal. I had never come to terms with the issue of physical healing. It was, and is, a subject of great contention in the church and the debate often left me scared and quite bewildered. People seemed to forget I was a real person as they used me more or less as a tool to prove or disprove their own theological viewpoint. Throughout my childhood I encountered many people who, insisting God wanted to heal me, would clap hands on my head, pray in some strange language and then cast out supposed demons.

But I never walked. I never improved. My sense of failure mounted and I came to dread meeting that sort of Christian. Such hurts, experienced over the years, made me very cynical and scathing about physical healing. And they left me with huge questions.

That morning I had finished my devotions before Kathy helped me into my clothes and wheeled me through to the kitchen for breakfast. Christian music was playing softly in the background as she skilfully manoeuvred my chair under the breakfast table.

Looking up to greet Uncle Ivan and Aunty Joyce, I stared in utter astonishment. For there, seated at the breakfast table, was Sam Breggs. My mouth dropped open and I blinked to ensure I wasn't seeing an apparition.

How could it be Sam? Hadn't he died a few months

back? Sam had been struck down with bowel cancer, and his condition had deteriorated rapidly. The last time I spoke with him he looked like a wizened old man instead of a rugged outdoor type in his early fifties. His back was hunched and his once large frame had become gaunt, with every bone and socket prominent. His movements, once vibrant, had become sluggish and painful.

He'd been given only six weeks to live. I had doubted he'd even live that long. I'd assumed he'd died during the week I'd been out of town on holiday. But here he was—not just alive and kicking, but tucking into a hearty breakfast with obvious enjoyment. I was dumbstruck. His presence scared and confused me. Was this a ghost from the past? But as Sam grinned at me across the table, I knew he wasn't a ghost. It was Sam Breggs, the genuine article. Before me was a living miracle—he'd been completely healed!

Kathy sat down beside me at the table, and the usually boisterous Bowen household fell silent. As Sam spoke to us a peace filled the room—the presence of God pervading everything and everybody. We were gripped with awe.

Aunty Joyce thoughtfully spooned cereal into my mouth as Sam began. But I was too emotionally choked to swallow food. I leaned forward in my chair, utterly absorbed by the conversation unfolding across the table. I wanted to reach over, to touch Sam. Perhaps the healing would rub off. Perhaps then God would touch me in the same way. Sam said that he'd been near death before going to a healing service led by an exuberant, tambourine-playing Englishman, evangelist Harry Greenwood.

'During the service I was called out for prayer,' he told his hushed audience. 'As he placed both hands on my head, an intense heat began to flow through my body. My knees buckled and I crumpled backwards. I couldn't remain upright. Caught by one of the ushers, they laid me gently on the floor where I stayed immobile for fifteen minutes, immersed in the presence of God.

'When I finally picked myself up off the floor, I was still in excruciating pain. It seemed nothing had happened. No healing had taken place.

'As I struggled back to my seat, there was a great deal of movement in the congregation as other people began to rise to their feet and claim their healing. Although still in pain, I wept and rejoiced as I began to catch a glimpse of the awesome love and power of God Almighty as he touched people. There was a beautiful presence of the Holy Spirit there that night. Tremendous heat continued to surge through my body, despite the terrible pain that I still felt as I left the building. I only just managed to get home without passing out.

When I reached home I staggered in through the door to the bathroom. For ten minutes the pain was unbelievable; ten minutes of physical hell.' His face contorted at the memory. 'My bowels burst—but I was rid of that life-threatening cancer.'

By the time Sam returned to the specialist, medical investigations found no trace of any cancer. All symptoms were gone. He walked out with a clean bill of health, and the medical profession declared him to be a living miracle.

'That's got to be the power of God,' he concluded.

My mind raced as I sat transfixed by his every word. Was God allowing me to hear of this wonderful healing as an indication that I too would be healed? Could he touch me like he'd touched Sam?

Suddenly, Sam looked intently at me and abruptly changed the subject to talk about his beloved wife, Sally, who had died just a year ago after a car accident. His voice trembled with emotion, showing that he was still working through his grief. 'Miracles and healings do uplift Christ,' he affirmed. 'However, I also believe suffering is not purposeless. God is teaching me that the only way to learn strong faith is to endure great trial. These pressured circumstances have developed in me precious faith otherwise unobtainable.' Eyes moist, he continued: 'Yes, I know Christ and the power of his resurrection and healing. But I know too a little of what it means to experience the fellowship of his suffering. Suffering is not accidental. The demonstration of the supernatural is powerful, but never forget, it's in the valleys that we grow—not on the mountain tops.'

I struggled to understand the depths of this conversation—all the talk about mountains and valleys. Why did a person need to experience the valleys to gain greater depth?

With these thoughts racing through my mind, Kathy silently wheeled me from the table back into the bedroom. Moments ticked by. I sat watching her excitedly preparing to meet her boyfriend who would be taking her to work. Her carefree manner vividly contrasted with my deeply reflective mood.

I felt a sudden surge of jealousy. It was wrong, I knew, and quite unfair on Kathy. But what chances were there of me ever being asked out by a man? She could get a job. She was free to go out. But I'd been turned down every time I tried to find work.

I knew that thinking like this was foolish. How could I compete with an able-bodied person? I struggled to control my feelings, and began to tell Kathy about a verse which I was grappling with: 'I will give you a new heart and put a new spirit in you; I will remove from you your heart of stone and give you a heart of flesh' (Ezek 36:26).

For many months I'd felt a stoniness in my relationship with God. I'd struggled long and hard yet was unable to overcome it. I desperately sought release, knowing this would launch me into what God wanted me to do in life. I reflected on the vision he had given me. What did he mean? What was his will? What was the appointed task?

'Maybe you'll experience a supernatural encounter similar to Sam's,' Kathy suggested tentatively. 'I wonder if God will heal you? Mind you, being able-bodied isn't all it's cracked up to be. Life has its trials and tribulations. We all get frustrated. It may be about different things, but it happens to us all.'

She hesitated, her brown eyes sparkling as she flashed me a smile. 'Don't you ever forget, I love you as you are!'

I giggled, and proceeded to tell her that only that morning my Bible reading had been about God speaking through an ass—Baalam's ass. 'If God can use an ass, he can use *anything*. God's not disabled, nor is he limited by disability. He expects us to use what we have—to concentrate on our abilities, not our disabilities.'

'Marg, you're a scream,' Kathy chuckled. 'That's certainly a challenge. We must not limit God. Perhaps one day you'll have a powerful ministry...a wheelchair ministry?'

I swallowed hard and didn't reply. Kathy was wrong. I would *never* accept ministry from a wheelchair. If God called me to preach, I would preach properly. I would stand tall, and then I would preach. But I would not minister from a wheelchair.

'Here, read this,' said Kathy. 'Kathryn Kuhlman's second book, *God Can Do It Again*.' Kathy thrust the book under my nose, unaware of my thoughts. 'Amazing testimonies—dynamic healings. I'd be interested in your comments.'

Then, almost before I could take it all in, she was off.

'Must dash,' she said, half out of the door. 'See you at tea time.'

Despite my bad experiences at healing meetings, I couldn't refute Sam's dynamic encounter with the power of God. I'd be a fool, now, to believe the contrary. So I squatted comfortably on the floor and fumbled to open the pages of the book Kathy had recommended.

I was immediately enthralled. I began to weep as I read story after story of God's healing love.

I was still reading when, late in the afternoon, Kathy burst into the room. 'Guess who's in town? How about we attend a Harry Greenwood meeting? Let's go to the Town Hall and see the action for ourselves,' she babbled excitedly.

This was too much. The man who'd prayed for Sam was in town that night. Could it be a coincidence, or was it God's timing?

We arrived early to be assured of a good seat. I'd only been settled a few minutes when I witnessed my second miracle that day. Tom Hadfield, a mechanic friend who wheeled me around at Bible class camps, raced up, threw his arms around me and affectionately pecked my cheek. Again, I stared in amazement. Tom had severely injured his spine when the bonnet of a car on which he'd been working crashed onto his back. His injuries weren't severe enough to warrant him being in a wheelchair, but the accident had left him disabled. He had walked with difficulty, often experiencing excruciating pain, and was forced to draw an invalid benefit.

Yet here he was in front of me, cheeks glowing, mischievously laughing as he bounced with agility and ease. He was a picture of health. Another friend healed by God!

I could no longer refute the reality of God's power —not now. I knew Sam and Tom well enough to be sure their stories weren't a hoax.

Having heard Tom's story, I agreed to be prayed for in private by Mr Greenwood before the meeting. Tension mounted as we entered the prayer room. As I strained to muster up faith, I felt Mr Greenwood nestle both his hands on my head. Electricity seemed to crackle from him. I leaned forward in my chair, expectant.

'No, don't strain,' his voice was soft, soothing. 'Don't try to be healed. You're not the one who does the healing. God is. Allow the Spirit of God to do the work.

'We had a young spastic man back in England. We prayed for him consistently for twelve months and a gradual healing took place. Last Christmas he left his chair—totally healed.

'Relax, rest in the Lord, don't strive. That's the key.' As he prayed I felt a warm tingle flow through my body, but there was no obvious improvement in my condition.

Returning to the meeting, expectation rose within me. The tingling sensation continued. On the platform, Mr Greenwood's charismatic personality was captivating. With vibrancy and enthusiasm he led the crowd in singing that amazing hymn: 'There's power in the blood, power in the blood. ...'

We sang it once, twice, three times, over and over. Each time the music and words seemed to pulsate in our very veins as well as our vocal cords. The atmosphere was electric. All over the building people were raising their hands in praise as they sang. There was freedom. Freedom to pour out one's heart to the Creator; to thank the Saviour; to receive the Holy Spirit. Freedom to be creative before the Lord.

As Mr Greenwood came forward to speak he called for a moment of silent prayer. 'There's power in the name of Jesus,' he said softly into the microphone. As he spoke, a deep holy hush settled over the 2,000 seated people. One could hear soft muted exclamations of 'Praise God', and 'Thank you, Jesus'.

He continued: 'We know, Father, that miracles are going to happen in this place tonight. We feel the blessed presence of the Holy Spirit. We promise to give you all the praise, all the glory, for what is about to happen here. Pour out your Spirit upon us, for Jesus' sake. ...'

Again Harry Greenwood addressed the audience: 'Let me tell you what happened several weeks ago back in England. I wish you could meet my friend Billy Moore. We were conducting a healing service and Billy had driven to this meeting all the way from a little village eighty miles west of Northampton, bringing with him four women, all of whom were crippled and one in a wheelchair.

'Not only was Billy healed of bleeding ulcers, but everyone who'd travelled in his car received a healing blessing. One of the ladies, a doctor's wife, had not found healing through medicine, but that night she found healing in Jesus.'

A ripple of praise flowed through the congregation, and again I heard people saying 'Praise God' and 'Hallelujah'.

'But wait,' Harry Greenwood continued, his voice more intense. 'That's not the most amazing thing. The amazing thing was that Billy went back, chartered a bus and brought a whole busload of people the next week. And since then it seems like half the population of this little town has been to our healing services.'

The congregation joined in laughing, praising and applauding God. Then he grew serious. His voice was low—he was almost whispering: 'There's a beautiful presence of the Holy Spirit here tonight. It must have been something like this in the early church when the Holy Spirit descended upon those Christians as they began to worship.

'The light of God's love is in this place. But it is dark outside and it's getting darker. There's so much hate out there, so much greed, so much misunderstanding. And the only hope is the love of God. That's why we are here tonight—to see the love and power of God at work.'

As I watched and listened to Harry preach, I was

struck by the love and faith emanating from him. His preaching was powerful, faith-building, yet thought-provoking. His message that evening was entitled 'Love Is the Key'.

'Never underestimate the power of love. There is tremendous power in love itself.' His voice rang loud and clear. 'I love God with every atom of my being. And I know that in this place tonight the Holy Spirit is moving...gently.'

Every eye was fixed on the lone figure centre stage. Every ear tuned. Even the coughing and movement in the seats had stopped. We were on holy ground.

I sat, transfixed. The sermon lasted an hour yet time passed in a flash.

Suddenly he pointed to the middle of the crowd. 'Somewhere over here, someone has just received a healing from asthma. I don't know who you are, but you came to this service wheezing with asthma and it has just disappeared.

'Somebody's ear has just opened. It happened not more than a minute ago.'

Harry Greenwood could not explain how he knew the persons and the illnesses of which they were healed. But he did. And the ushers knew that when he reported a healing there was a healing.

'I know these things,' he'd say. 'but I do not pretend to understand why or how I know, except that God speaks them into my mind.'

Now there was a great deal of movement in the congregation as people began to rise to their feet and declare their healing, reaching out in thanks to God.

I sat with my heart pounding. 'Lord, what next? Who's next?' Harry continued. 'Diabetes is being healed. To my right, someone is being healed of diabetes. Don't be afraid—the heat in your body is supernatural.

'A growth, a tumour, has disappeared from the back of someone's neck. A person, at the back of the congregation, feel the back of your neck. You'll find the lump has gone.

'An extreme case of sinusitis has been instantly healed...a blind eye is clearing and vision is being restored right now as I speak...There's a heart being healed. A man with a heart that was more dead than alive has just been healed. And there's an elderly man, down here some place,' he gestured to the left, 'who's being healed of a painful prostrate gland. That operation won't be necessary. God has taken care of it right now.

'Oh, there's so much power here tonight,' he exclaimed. 'It's everywhere. It's so strong I can hardly stand.'

Groups of people gathered in both aisles to tell how they'd just been healed. Harry Greenwood wandered about with a microphone allowing people the opportunity to praise God and declare his wonders.

Some said that they had been sitting just where Harry indicated and had been healed of the exact disease he described.

He put both hands on people's heads and began to pray: 'Lord Jesus, so fill this person with your love and power. ...'

There was no hysteria. People were being genuinely touched. One man's knees buckled and he crumpled backwards. He was caught by an usher and gently laid on the floor. Kathy looked towards me. She'd explained to me earlier that she was thrilled to witness genuine healings, but was still confused by 'the falling under the power'. As our eyes met, she shook her head and shrugged her shoulders.

A gasp went up from the congregation. Harry placed both hands on one person, then another and another. Each person collapsed onto the floor and lay bathed in the presence of God.

Then a young woman came forward for prayer. She was weeping profusely.

'What is it?' Harry Greenwood asked.

'I want to be saved...to be born again,' she sobbed.

'Healing is marvellous,' Harry continued, 'but the greatest miracle is the transformation of a soul from darkness to light. I do not care if I never see another body healed as long as I know there are souls being saved. Physical healing is nothing compared to the healing of a soul.'

I sensed he was deliberately pointing the service towards a climax.

'I believe the blood of Jesus is sufficient atonement for sin,' he declared in ringing tones. 'If you've never been born again, if you've never experienced the joy of salvation, the knowledge that your sins are forgiven —if you've never made a total commitment of your life to God's Son, Jesus Christ, I want you to do it now!'

Jesus said: 'Him that cometh to me I will in no wise cast out.' And they came! Elderly, middle-aged people, teenagers. Some were in tears. Others had shining faces. Some walked quickly, their jaws set as though afraid if they hesitated they might change their minds. Others plodded, seemingly weighed down by heavy burdens. The aisles overflowed with people.

'We couldn't possibly pronounce a benediction on a service such as this,' Harry said to those who remained in their seats. 'All I can say is as you go, rejoice at the marvellous things God has done in this place tonight.'

The crowd turned reluctantly to leave. Some remained standing in their places, their faces lifted up to God, absorbed in prayer. Others, perfect strangers, were exchanging greetings.

The elderly man who'd been healed of the painful prostrate gland was standing in the aisle looking around in awe and wonder. 'Isn't it wonderful!' he exclaimed. 'The love—you can feel it in this place, can't you?'

I nodded, too emotionally choked to answer. But he

was right. I'd never experienced a meeting like it. I thought of the years I had spent in churches where people scorned the idea that God was dead, yet acted as if they were at his funeral service every Sunday.

Dozens of names flashed through my mind—disabled friends, fellow Christians, sceptics, loved ones. How I wished they could have shared this experience with me. I didn't want to leave—somehow things still felt unfinished. I gazed once more up at the stage. Suddenly everything changed—almost like a dream, yet undoubtedly real. I watched as a beautiful young woman danced on to the platform. She wore a stunning yellow dress, with a dainty pearl necklace and white shoes. Every part of her body was perfect, totally co-ordinated!

I stared. That young woman was me. In my hand I held a microphone and I preached with the same power and authority of some of the great male evangelists of the day.

I could not believe it. I stood tall. My mind and emotions grappled with the vision. Nothing is too difficult for God. A snap of his fingers and this vision could be reality!

So near yet so far. It was agonising as I tried to interpret the vision. It must mean one of two things: healing here on earth, or wholeness in heaven. The problem was, I could recall no scriptures referring to yellow dresses in heaven. And I had an identical yellow dress in my wardrobe back home!

I lay in bed that night, still supercharged by the events of the day: Sam's dramatic healing, Kathryn Kuhlman's book and her ministry, Tom's story, Harry Greenwood and that amazing meeting. My whole system was taut with wonder. Sleep was impossible.

I believed God wanted me to dream big dreams, to have wild expectations of what he wanted to do in and through my life. He wanted my co-operation in bringing that vision to birth in a tangible form.

'God,' I prayed, 'you can do anything, *anything* you want with me!'

Little did I realise then the far-reaching implications of such a prayer.

I scrambled out of bed and, squatting on the floor, began to read once more the book *God Can Do It Again*. As I read, tremendous heat again surged through my body. I began to shake, then sob. The sobbing was so intense I crumpled onto the floor, my face buried in the carpet. Never before had I experienced such dynamic power. As I lay there—helpless but willing—it was as if the Master Surgeon was carving open my life and literally taking out my heart of stone and putting a heart of flesh in its place. I knew I would never be the same again, and my life would no longer be my own.

I had now moved from a position of merely being slightly curious about the power of the Holy Spirit, to a place in which I bowed the knee in reverence to his holiness and sovereignty.

My experience wasn't dissimilar to those described in the Bible—people like Moses, Isaiah, the apostle Paul and Mary the mother of Jesus. They all had meetings with God, supernatural encounters that were deeply emotional and unnerving events.

How long I lay there, immersed in the presence of God, I do not know. When I finally tumbled into bed, I sobbed myself into an exhausted sleep.

When I awoke next morning, the euphoria remained. I pulled my Bible towards me and began to read. References tumbled out of the pages, one after another, almost as if they were written in capital letters and bright red ink. They all endorsed everything I'd learned and experienced the previous day.

Romans 4: 20–21, 'Yet he did not waver through unbelief regarding the promise of God, but was strengthened in his faith and gave glory to God, being fully persuaded that God had power to do what he had promised.'

Hebrews 10:23, 'Let us hold unswervingly to the hope we profess, for he who promised is faithful.'

Luke 1:37, 'For nothing is impossible with God.'

Luke 1:45, 'Blessed is she who has believed that what the Lord has said to her will be accomplished.'

The message was loud and clear, confirmed by scripture after scripture: I must be healed—and *soon*! Then I would do great exploits for God.

5
God's Green Light

As the days went by, I believed God would heal me, and my desire to be bodily co-ordinated led me to claim apparently iron-clad promises in the Bible. Surely I was over the learning phase of my disability; now was the time to move on to the next phase—healing.

After all, I reasoned, God allows us to experience sickness and suffering in order to teach us, and I believed I had learned an enormous amount through my disability. My scepticism regarding healing had now turned to belief. I'd be a fool to believe otherwise. Sam Breggs and Tom Hadfield were living proof of the power of God to reverse permanent, incurable and terminal diseases.

My spiritual life blossomed as my faith grew. I yearned to know God more intimately and developed an insatiable hunger for his word, particularly the accounts of the miracles in the New Testament. They came alive with new significance.

One which never ceased to thrill me was the man lame from birth who was laid daily beside the gate Beautiful. Peter and John passed by. The man asked for alms and received his legs! I prayed with enthusiasm and conviction that God would give me legs too.

It was April 1974, and winter was rapidly approaching. Despite my high spirits and buoyant faith, my

physical health was at an ebb. As I sat on the couch,
meditating on a Bible passage, a message flickered
through my brain. At first it was a passing thought,
but then it became a persistent niggle. Repeatedly it
dictated to my mind: 'Look in the challenge.'

I knew the message was referring to *Challenge
Weekly,* New Zealand's national Christian newspaper, a
copy of which was lying on the floor.

Curious, I scrambled over to it, and as the paper
splayed open, I saw Kathryn Kuhlman beckoning to
me from one of the pages. Arms outstretched, the
invitation was as personal as if she'd been standing
right there in the room. It was as if she was compelling
me to reach out and come to America.

How I agonised over that message. What was God
saying? Why Kathryn Kuhlman? America was half the
world away.

Still confused, I determined to write to her, carefully
explaining my situation—the yellow dress, preaching,
chosen for an appointed task. Maybe she was considering coming to New Zealand, or Australia, to conduct
miracle services. Even if she wasn't, perhaps she would
consider coming—just for me! I was convinced God
wanted me healed, and it seemed that Miss Kuhlman
would be the vessel he would use. I was determined to
attend at least one of her services, and was prepared to
crawl over glass in order to do so. Nothing and nobody
would stop me.

For weeks after posting my letter I was on tenter-
hooks. Each day I half-expected, half-feared her reply.
Would she receive my letter? Would she reject my
suggestion of her coming to New Zealand or Australia?
How many thousands of letters identical to mine did
she receive? Would mine be overlooked, perhaps filed
in the rubbish bin?

Despite my conviction that God wanted to heal
everyone, I rationalised my own lack of progress to
God's timing. After all, I reasoned, God's timing

for me would be when Kathryn Kuhlman conducted healing services in New Zealand.

Six weeks later Miss Kuhlman's reply arrived. I held it, heart palpitating, almost too scared to open it, for its contents would have the potential either to dash or raise my hopes. Excitement and anxiety battled inside. Finally I took a deep breath and ripped open the envelope.

The news was disappointing. Miss Kuhlman had received several invitations from Australia and New Zealand, but had no immediate plans to accept. Her schedule for the next two years was already fully booked. She did point me, however, to a Bible passage which encouraged me not to look at the forces against me, but at the resources in God available to conquer the impossible and to travel to America and attend services at the Shrine.

My initial disappointment faded. 'All things are possible with God,' she had encouraged. I believed that too, and my mind began to race. Maybe I could go to America. Why not step out in faith? The obstacles loomed large. How would I finance such a trip? Who would be available to accompany me? Would I physically cope with such a venture? What about accommodation? Despite these hurdles, something deep within me kept urging me on to pursue the impossible.

By the time I next saw Kathy, I was in a state of high excitement, and enthusiastically told her of my plans, which were becoming grander by the minute.

'I'm going to America, I know I am,' I babbled. 'I'm going to be healed, I've got to be. . . .'

Kathy appeared unmoved. 'Look, Marg, I'm excited for you. But don't let this whole thing get out of hand. Are you sure it isn't wishful thinking, that you are not twisting God's arm, blackmailing him? You must be realistic about this. God won't be manipulated.'

I was taken aback, even angry at Kathy's negativity.

She'd always been most supportive, believing that God could and would heal me. Why change now?

What I couldn't see behind her negative comments were her motives. She had seen me hurt too often by well-meaning Christians. She'd seen the great pressure imposed on me by healing services—and the guilt, condemnation, the sense of failure I experienced when I did not rise to people's expectations and leave my chair. Kathy was troubled. She did not want me to go to America full of high hopes only to be hurt again. She feared that eventually all these factors would destroy me—for a person can only take so much.

Good as her intentions were, however, at that moment they seemed unnecessary and unhelpful. Why wasn't she fanning the flame of my faith for this great odyssey?

'I'm absolutely convinced God wants me healed,' I told her, a little more reticent now. 'He wants us healthy and able so we can best serve him. I don't want to spend an entire lifetime in a wheelchair, feeling a deficient woman.'

Kathy walked over and knelt gently at my chair. Her tall slender body folded before me, her sparkling brown eyes now fired with concern as she took my hands in hers and devotedly said, 'I would give my own legs to see you walk.'

'Yeah,' I muttered unhelpfully, still annoyed.

Then she began to tell me a story. 'There was a man with an incurable ailment. His neighbour bargained with God that on the day he witnessed a miracle he would commit his life to Christ. God took him at his word, and healed the man's ailment. The whole neighbourhood heard about the miracle. For a week the streets were abuzz over the work of God. But almost as quickly as it happened, everyone forgot again. The man who made the bargain with God never did fulfil his part of the bargain. Today he is still a non-believer.

'If you believe your healing is going to rock this

town, you could be disappointed,' Kathy concluded. 'You too could finish up nothing more than a five-day wonder. Think about it.'

She recounted how Mark's Gospel recorded several miracles. Jesus knew full well that the miracles in Moses' and Elijah's day attracted crowds, but rarely encouraged long-term faithfulness. He brought a hard message of obedience and sacrifice, not a side-show for sensation-seekers.

'Sure enough,' Kathy went on, 'the true sceptics of Jesus' day—much like people today—explained away his power. If God's voice spoke from heaven, some dismissed it as thunder. Others credited his gift to Satan. And Jesus' staunchest enemies refused to trust him even when faced with solid evidence, such as the words of the blind man: 'One thing I do know. I was blind—but now I see!' They threw insults at the healed man and threw him out of court. When Lazarus showed up alive after four days in the tomb, they even tried to kill him off again.

'The Bible shows that miracles—dramatic, show-stopping ones, like many of us still long for—simply don't foster deep faith. Look at the account of the Transfiguration when Jesus' face shone like the sun and his clothes became dazzling, whiter than anyone in the world could bleach them. To the disciples' astonishment, two long-dead giants of Jewish history, Moses and Elijah, appeared in the cloud with them. God spoke audibly. It was too much to take; the disciples literally freaked out and fell to the ground, terrified.

'Why does a God who has the power to right what is wrong sometimes choose not to? Why did Jesus bother with miracles at all? Why heal one paralysed man at Bethesda—but only one?

'Boy, have I got a lot of questions I'm going to ask God one day when I get to heaven,' Kathy exclaimed.

Her message was penetrating: 'Accepting disability

does not necessarily mean lack of faith. It can, in fact, be an act of faith.'

Kathy sensed my inner turmoil and frustration. Tears weren't too far away. 'Don't be one-track minded, Marg,' she warned. 'I'm not wanting to put a damper on your faith, or your healing, but there are two sides to the issue.' She hesitated, 'You know, maybe you've got greater credibility in your chair than if you were out of it. Maybe it's an even greater indication of God's power.'

'What do you mean?' I asked, reluctantly allowing her to pursue her line of thought.

'Well, a physical healing would be like an explosive release of God's power in getting you out of your chair, but staying in the chair takes power too—controlled power flowing through you that makes it possible for you to cope.'

There was an awkward silence. What Kathy was saying made sense. Both types of power were part of the purposes of God.

'C'mon, enough,' Kathy broke my quiet. 'No more sermons. Let's go out.'

Jumping up off the floor, she grabbed a hair brush, raked it through my hair, examined my make-up, quickly touched it up and off we went.

I was tired by the time we arrived home, but my weariness quickly vanished as I answered the already ringing telephone. It was Molly Willette, a friend from Auckland, asking if I was still interested in going to a Kathryn Kuhlman service.

Molly was the mother of a multi-handicapped daughter. She had attended several miracle services at the Shrine Auditorium and seen Miss Kuhlman in action. She'd shared with me thrilling accounts of healing, as well as some deep disappointments.

Molly's husband worked for Air New Zealand and she was able to travel to America very cheaply on the staff discount scheme. So she volunteered to escort me to America, but because of her family commitments she would need to return to New Zealand within a few days. But the cost was prohibitive—$2,000, a sum totally out of the question on my disabled benefit. So I shelved the idea.

In the weeks and months that followed, it was as though Kathryn Kuhlman—or God—wouldn't let go of me. Suddenly, everything began to gather momentum. A miracle outside of my own will and control occurred.

My sister, Helen, who had been living in England for the last three years, was now being transferred to Boston to work as a Nanny. I wrote to her about the possibility of my going to Los Angeles, and explained my predicament. Her answer was prompt. At the end of her contract she would extend her visa and be in LA by March for six weeks. She would be available to me in whatever capacity I required.

Meanwhile, Miss Kuhlman and I continued to correspond. I'd send a 'prayer handkerchief' for her and her staff to pray over, and when it returned I would wear it, tied to my body. However, despite the way everything was dove-tailing, I felt there was one more confirmation I needed—direct revelation from God. I needed more than circumstantial evidence. I didn't want to take God's arm and twist it up his back. I needed God's green light—and urgently. To embark on such a journey without his approval would have been disastrous.

I began to fast and pray. After two days without food, I was virtually exhausted. I became more and more desperate. The answer must come, and soon. I pleaded for God to reveal his will—and he did.

It was mid-morning when I collapsed into a chair with my Bible open. As I glanced down it was as though one particular verse was highlighted, covered with a soft light. It read: 'I will put my Spirit in you and you will live, and I will settle you in your own land.

Then you will know that I the Lord have spoken and I have done it.' (Ezek 37:14).

'Lord,' I questioned, 'what do you promise?'

Just a couple of hours later God answered that question loud and clear. In the post that day was a small parcel containing a book. As the wrapping paper fell away from the cover, I let out an astonished gasp. I couldn't believe my eyes.

The title hit me almost physically—*10,000 Miles for a Miracle*. It was an account of a dramatic healing an Australian woman experienced while attending one of the Kathryn Kuhlman miracle services. Her story of travelling to America in pursuit of healing was identical to my situation—it was mind-boggling. And the book had been sent to me by a woman who had no idea I was contemplating such a trip myself. Her brief note read: 'I felt this little book was for you as a means of confirmation. Be encouraged. God's got it all under control.'

The woman whom the book was about had travelled 10,000 miles for her miracle, and New Zealand was about the same distance away. I relaxed. I was on the right track. My excitement grew daily. And the miracle continued to unfold.

A new pricing structure meant I could travel to America for a third of the original air fare. People spontaneously began to give me money, either pushing it into my hand or posting it to me. Before long my ticket and all expenses were provided for.

The obstacles that had once loomed large were now non-existent. So Molly and I booked our seats to Los Angeles. Red letter day was 20th March 1975. I had less than five months to wait—less than five months till I was healed!

The reactions of Christians to my plans differed widely. The church I was attending supported me fully, showing me tremendous love and support. Church members continued to pray for me regularly and believed with me for my healing, but they weren't embarrassed by the wheelchair either. They pledged to set up a prayer vigil when I was in America.

These were difficult days for my mother and father. Their church background had taught against healing, and they struggled hard to come to terms with my touring half-way round the world in search of a miracle. They were often misunderstood and suffered snide remarks, mainly from people who didn't understand the situation or the disabled. My mother, for so long burdened with caring for me, was at her wits' end. She'd tried every avenue possible to see me helped—therapists, institutions, chiropractors and specialists. Nothing had worked. During the lead-up to my trip away, she completely relinquished me to God. It was up to him, she decided. I was now God's responsibility. As far as she was concerned, any improvement or progress with my co-ordination or speech would be a miracle.

Many fellow Christians stood aloof, not knowing what to say, afraid I would fall flat on my face. Their attitude was best summed up by a conversation I overheard between two elders as I sat outside the church office.

'Why doesn't God roll up his sleeves and walk into this situation with power?' He hesitated a moment, then continued, 'If that girl rose out of her chair, it would rock this church!'

'I'm not sure about that,' retorted the other. 'What you hanker for today—signs and wonders—did nothing to instil lasting faith in the Israelites! Why is it that Christians yearn for a world with miracles and spectacular signs of God's power? Would miracles in this church really nourish our faith? Some people might credit them to the work of Satan. Perhaps signs and wonders would cause us to become addicted to signs, not lead us to God.'

'That's true, but wouldn't it be marvellous if Margie did rise out of her chair?' the elder persisted.

'Look, what if she's not healed? What if the girl is devastated, perhaps destroyed completely?'

'But what if she's healed?'

'*That*, dear brother, remains to be seen!'

6

Kathryn Kuhlman

Molly anxiously scanned my ghost-like face, worry etched on her brow. 'Are you going to make it, Marg?' she asked somewhat desperately. 'Are you all right?'

The eighteen-hour flight from Auckland to Los Angeles is a tiring experience for a fit and able-bodied person, but for me it proved a terrible physical ordeal. I struggled to breathe in the unnatural atmosphere of the pressurised cabin and could feel strength draining from my body. My physical discomfort was compounded by a stomach ulcer, which had left me weaker than usual. On that flight there were times when I too wondered when the trauma would end.

But the physical trauma wasn't the worst. The emotional roller-coaster I took on that plane journey was almost unbearable. Again and again I went over the miracles which had occurred to get me on that plane. I repeatedly recited to myself the scriptures I had been given as I tried to reassure myself that everything was fine, and that I would be healed. Excitement, and even a little fear, mounted, stretching my nerves to breaking point.

Despite our fears, we finally arrived in Los Angeles. It was an emotional moment for me as I was reunited with my sister, Helen, for the first time in five years. What a time of joy as we laughed and hugged each other.

Helen had arrived in Los Angeles a few days before Molly and I, and had spent the time scouting around the city to find suitable accommodation—a place within our financial means which also had easy access for my wheelchair.

After settling in, our first priority was to ascertain details of the miracle service the next day. We were advised to arrive no later than 8.30 am. The service would begin at 1 pm. We had to be willing to queue for hours to get a good seat.

We settled down for the night, but sleep wouldn't come. My mind raced as I lay there. Tomorrow might be the day, the day the prison that was my body would be unlocked. Tomorrow I might walk, run, dance. Tomorrow I might become normal.

Finally I fell asleep, but only for about four hours. Anything more was impossible as I was taut with excitement, hope and more than a little apprehension.

In the morning we turned on the television and the first thing we saw was Kathryn Kuhlman's programme. I studied her in her long pink gown, hanging on her every move, her every word. And all the time my mind was building up faith—preparing for my special moment.

As we ate breakfast, Helen reached across the table to butter my toast and cut it up and said, 'Do you know, that could be the last time I do that for you?'

My heart leapt. This was the day! This was the greatest day of my life! I was going to be normal!

The 8,000-seat Shrine Auditorium was a thirty-minute taxi ride from the hotel. As we drove through the streets of LA, I was full of apprehension. I didn't know what to expect. How would I handle myself when I finally got out of my chair? Who would be the first person I would ring back home? What would 'normal' be like?

I was also apprehensive about the extent of my healing that day. I didn't expect to receive the full dose

at the first meeting—that would come at a second
Kathryn Kuhlman meeting, when I would wear my
yellow dress and the vision would be fulfilled.

However, I was certain there would at least be an
improvement in my condition during the meeting. It
would be the beginning of total health. But where
would the improvement come? Would it be my voice,
my arms, my legs? There were so many possibilities for
improvement in my uncontrollable body.

We arrived at the Shrine and lined up near the front
of the queue. Many people had already gathered, some
had even slept on the steps overnight to be sure of a
seat.

Eventually, about 400 people in wheelchairs and
their attendants queued up at the huge side doors,
waiting to be let in to their specially-appointed seats.

Shortly after Helen and I had settled into line,
an ambulance—siren blaring and lights flashing—
screamed up to the doors. My heart jumped, thinking
someone had died. But it wasn't that. They pulled a
corpse-like figure out of the ambulance and she too
joined the queue on her stretcher. I realised that only a
miracle could help people like her and me.

As we waited and looked around, I was struck by the
utter hopelessness of the people there. They were the
people shunned by society, the broken and crippled.
There was a look of despair in so many eyes. Their
whole being spoke of the rejection and pain that came
with serious disability. I couldn't comprehend that
amount of human suffering in one place.

Yet there was something else as well, something
more intangible. It was a fire that wouldn't go out, a
hope beyond hope that today would be the end of their
misery. People were straining for an unseen hand to
reach down and touch them.

At about 9.30 a group of ushers began moving down
the rows of wheelchairs, and each of us received a tag
—either red, white, green or yellow. Mine was red,

meaning I couldn't leave my chair. We reds were the most handicapped of all.

And as they moved down the line one of them confirmed to me what I fervently believed already. I was going to be healed. As she tagged the wheelchairs, she turned to me, finger pointed, and said, 'There's power here, honey. Begin thanking him, stop asking him.'

Immediately, another turned and said of me, 'She's a chosen person.'

Helen and I hurriedly looked around. No one else had received such a word. No one else had been encouraged like that. We began to thank God for the healing which we were certain must come.

A camaraderie, fostered by the wonderful ushers, developed as we sat waiting for the massive doors to open. The air buzzed with expectancy. Who would be the ones who would rise that day from their chairs? It was exciting to realise that so many of us would soon shake loose the shackles from our bodies. I wondered who else would join me in testifying on Kathryn Kuhlman's stage. The word from that usher had confirmed everything I knew to be true. God had brought me to Los Angeles to be healed.

I gradually became aware that there were some people around me who were cynical and critical. Despite the wonderful example of the ushers and the testimonies of many who had been to previous services, they scoffed at the thought of God healing today. They didn't believe in God, they said, and cursed and blasphemed. Some openly challenged God to heal them if he could. Others had only come at the insistence of a Christian friend.

I pitied those poor people. I thought that their attitude and lack of faith ruined any chance of their being healed. Perhaps that day they would commit their lives to Christ. After salvation, after true repentance, only then, perhaps, would they receive a miracle.

One man in particular attracted my attention. Crippled with arthritis, he was drinking whisky heavily to relieve his agony. Puffing furiously at a cigar he cursed God through the pain. I'd never heard such an extended vocabulary—the air was thick with profanities. I pitied yet condemned that man. I felt sorry for his incredible pain, yet reacted strongly against him for cursing God. He had no right to be healed, I thought. Not with an attitude like that.

As I sat there, I went through my verses of Scripture again, and thought about the miracles that had taken place to get me here and of the prophetic word given to me by those ushers. Yes, I was a chosen one all right.

At 11 am the huge doors were pulled back and the army of wheelchairs was slowly taken in. As I entered the Shrine I caught a glimpse of what I thought heaven would be like. The walls were hung with rich velvet and starry chandeliers sparkled from the ceiling which seemed to disappear into some unknown world.

I was led to a box which had room for twelve disabled people. It had a fantastic view of the stage and the whole auditorium. How wonderfully everything was falling into place. I couldn't have found a better place if I'd tried.

It took an hour and a half to get all the wheelchairs in place. Once again, the ushers showed tremendous patience—with painstaking care they would arrange a line of wheelchairs just right, and then someone in the middle would wreck it all by having to get out to go to the toilet.

High up in my position above the other wheelchair patients, I nestled back to watch the goings on. Helen was sitting behind my box, close enough to help if needed. I looked down and noticed the cursing arthritic doubled up in a chair beneath me. My heart went out to him, without really knowing how to respond. The man had such great needs, but his language incensed me.

The choir, in magnificent robes, were already in position, practising their songs. Every now and then Kathryn Kuhlman herself would come out, just dressed in ordinary clothes. She would talk to the choir, disappear, then return again.

I had only just settled down and begun taking in the atmosphere when I was interrupted by a smiling usher. 'Honey,' he said, 'you are going to require my attention during the service. I'll have to shift you.'

I protested strongly, pointing out that I didn't need medication or toileting. But he patiently explained that he had another reason for moving me.

'God has told me you're the one to be healed,' he said. 'The Lord is going to do a work on you, honey. You're the one to be healed and you may need ministering to. It will be easier for both of us if I change your position.'

I didn't want to delay my healing, so I obediently went where he wanted me. And as he walked away I went through my mental check-list again. There were the scriptures, the vision, the miracles to get me there and now these people telling me I was chosen, that I would be healed. My emotions were mixed, but the tide of excitement was steadily rising.

The usher returned soon after and said, 'You have a wonderful work for Jesus ahead of you. Do you know that? You are going to speak to crowds of people, to be a witness before large congregations. Do you have a desire to work for the Lord? Do you know the Lord?

'The Lord has spoken to me through a word of knowledge that you are to be a prophetess of love. Hundreds of people are going to be blessed by your ministry.'

And then he told me to begin to reach out for the healing which was surely mine.

'We must concentrate on your speech,' he said. 'Let's believe God. Start repeating, "I love you, Jesus. Thank you, Jesus. Praise you, Jesus."'

And in my garbled, semi-intelligible way, I tried to get my tongue around the words. I began to thank Jesus, love him and praise him. I concentrated on my wayward mouth and tongue, striving to receive this initial healing to my vocal cords.

The usher crouched with me, repeating the words with me over and over again. We recited our words of thanks and praise ten times, then twenty times, then fifty, then 100 and soon it seemed like we had been repeating them thousands and thousands of times, over and over again.

'I love you, Jesus. Thank you, Jesus. Praise you, Jesus. ...'

At noon the main doors opened and a tidal wave of humanity surged into the Shrine. They poured down the aisles and within twenty minutes every seat was filled. The heavenly auditorium began to throb with expectancy as the magic hour—1 pm—neared. The orchestra was playing, the choir was singing, bodies leaned forward in seats, eyes became riveted to the stage, whispers rippled through the congregation, 'She's coming. ...'

The choir launched into 'Because he lives' and then 'He touched me'.

At last, dressed in her shimmering white gown, Miss Kuhlman swept onto the stage. Every eye, every nerve end focused sharply on that solitary figure. The entire auditorium exploded as people roared and clapped. They loved her. Some, including me, even worshipped her.

All around me people rose, spontaneously raising their arms towards heaven, voices blending together in a marvellous symphony of praise. The whole building filled with music. It swelled from the main floor below me, and vibrated from the walls and ceiling.

Amid the excitement, I glanced below to see how my cursing arthritic friend was responding. To my astonishment I saw him standing absolutely straight, arms held high, and tears streaming down his face. He was prancing from leg to leg and waving his arms about.

'I don't believe it,' he cried out. 'I don't believe in God.'

And then, inevitably, he changed his mind.

'Oh yes I do. Yes I do. He's real, he's real. I'm healed, I'm healed. God have mercy.' He was hysterical with joy.

I was to see him again a month later at the next service. He was on the platform with all his medical records as proof of the dramatic healing—a totally changed man, physically and spiritually.

An early highlight of the meeting was when Miss Kuhlman, who knew from my letters that I would be there that day, introduced me to the crowd.

'We have a young lady here from New Zealand,' she proclaimed. 'God bless you. Where are you?'

It took them a while to find me, but when they did, Miss Kuhlman urged the audience to 'give her a big "God bless you"'. The organ chimed, the bells rang and I beamed.

Miracles, such as the arthritic man's began immediately. As soon as Miss Kuhlman stepped onto the stage people were healed.

One woman burst onto the platform. She had had both her breasts removed after twelve cysts had been discovered in each one. Now, miraculously, both breasts had grown back as she sat in that service. After testifying of this wonderful event, the woman disappeared and returned about an hour later with a reluctant doctor from a Los Angeles hospital. She had driven across town to produce proof of the healing. He came to the microphone and Miss Kuhlman said to him, 'Did this woman have cancer and both breasts removed?'

'Yes.'

'Did you perform the surgery?'

'Yes.'

'Then what has happened here today?'

He wouldn't say the word 'miracle', but as Miss Kuhlman pointed out, that woman now had the same 'feminine body contours' as any other woman, so she answered for the tongue-tied doctor: 'It's a miracle then.'

The stream of people healed seemed to be endless. Their stories were inspiring and wonderful. Some jumped, some danced, some ran, and the crowd seethed with excitement.

But in my little box, perched above most of the audience, something in my heart had turned cold. The minute Miss Kuhlman had walked on to the stage I knew something was wrong. I could, without doubt, feel the presence of God with me right there in that meeting. But I knew something was missing—and that was his healing touch on my life. Healing was all around, but it was out there, out in the audience. Somehow I sensed that it wasn't inside me, it wasn't touching me.

'Reach out, and take whatever there is,' Miss Kuhlman said. 'Hold on to it and receive healing.' I reached out with everything I had, but there was nothing to take. The coldness increased as my usher friend encouraged me throughout the service.

'C'mon, honey. Tell him you love him. Start now, "I love you, Jesus. ..."' And so we began to recite again and again, 'I love you, Jesus. Thank you, Jesus. Praise you, Jesus.'

I was puzzled and confused. No such demands were placed on the other eleven in my box. He prayed for no one else except me. All around the auditorium people were being healed when nobody even prayed for them. They just rose up and walked! On and on we prayed. I launched into thanking God, then praising him. Periodically he would lay his hands on me, command satanic powers to come under control and order demons out of my body. An hour passed. Then another. Then another. In all we prayed for five hours!

Around me the service continued unabated, but by now I was only vaguely aware of what was happening. I didn't even hear Miss Kuhlman's message, so intent was I on stretching my faith to receive the long-awaited and promised healing.

The longer we continued to work on my voice, the more tired I became and the worse my words slurred, slipping back into my usual cerebral palsied drawl.

I wanted to scream at the usher, to tell him something was wrong. I wanted to scream at the crowd, all so engrosed in the meeting and the healings. I wanted to scream at God. Something was wrong and he wasn't doing anything. Nothing made sense. The more I tried, the worse I became.

Sometimes we would take five- or ten-minute breaks, during which I tried desperately to regain my strength to launch into another round of thanking the Lord for non-existent healing.

In these breaks I also managed to monitor the continuation of the service. Often people would come to the platform with a bag of drugs or a built-up shoe, and Miss Kuhlman would take them and spin round and round, whirling them in the air before throwing them to a row of doctors sitting in front of the stage. There were gales of laughter and tears of joy at the excitement of God at work.

After testifying to their healings, those coming off the platform would return to their seats and often others who hadn't been healed would reach across the aisles to stop them and touch them, hoping the power of God might somehow rub off.

Amid the euphoria, however, my life was breaking apart. No one seemed to be aware of my struggle. Their miracles seemed so simple. Why was I finding it such a great struggle, such a frustrating ordeal? Why was the usher pestering me? Why did he go on and on with my speech? Why couldn't I just get up and be healed? Why couldn't God just take over my tongue? What's normal, anyway? Was I possessed by a demon? The disappointment and frustration seeped deep down inside me.

At last, the service ended. It was about 5 pm, nearly nine hours after Helen and I had first arrived.

It was devastating to realise that after all that effort I was actually worse than when I had arrived. I was absolutely exhausted—physically, emotionally and spiritually drained. There hadn't even been partial healing, nothing to give me hope.

As the service drew to a close, I summoned my dwindling strength and made one last effort to reach out and receive healing. I looked down at Miss Kuhlman. With her reddish-brown hair and long white gown she looked to me like Jesus.

So I reached out to Jesus. I strained upwards for my healing and it was then I heard an almost audible voice, which I knew was God: 'You will never leave that wheelchair until you have gone through things so deep you will never forget them. I have chosen you, and you are in the furnace of affliction. Through suffering I will refine you as silver. You are mine. For my own sake, my own glory I will do this.'

I slumped back, more confused than ever. I didn't understand the message and didn't understand why I had to wait. Everything seemed so right.

Soon after it was all over. Miss Kuhlman had an altar call declaring that there was no greater miracle than being born again. Hundreds poured forward to commit their lives to Christ. Everyone was delirious. But I was crushed.

The usher who had prayed with me for all those hours was totally perplexed.

'Well, are you going to come through today or not?' he asked, seeming to imply that it was somehow my fault. 'Come on, don't go away disappointed. Try again.'

So I launched into saying, 'I love you, Jesus' another twenty or thirty times before the pressure became too much and I crumbled into an exhausted heap.

It was over and I was no different. Around me I sensed a series of similar reactions. No one in my box had been healed. Twelve broken and battered bodies went in at the start of the service, and twelve broken and battered bodies went out at the end. Sadness emanated from the box. The gurgling of the drain of the unconscious woman (the one who had been brought in the ambulance soon after I arrived at the Shrine) continued. Sobs began to break out from devastated people as they realised that their dreams hadn't been fulfilled.

As Helen arrived to take me away, the usher had one last thought. 'I have never been wrong yet,' he said to Helen. 'She's the one. There will be a great improvement. It could happen on the way home. God bless you.'

Then he was gone.

Helen and I were left to make our way out of the heavenly Shrine Auditorium, trying to cope with our shattered dreams.

'Don't crack and break in front of them,' Helen whispered fiercely. 'Control yourself, Marg, control your emotions. There's others worse. Put on a brave face.'

The brave act worked to some extent, but my face was badly twisted and it took a real effort not to cry. My head pounded from a headache and the words of the usher raced through my mind.

It remained more or less intact until we returned to the hotel. Then all the pent-up tension and frustration poured out as I repeatedly pounded my fist into the pillow.

'Why, God, why? You promised.'

7

A Vision Failed

During the next few weeks I wondered if I was losing my sanity. Helen and I stumbled through a nightmare of emotions. The crush of disappointment following the miracle service threatened to destroy me far quicker than cerebral palsy ever had.

At one stage, frantic, I went to a church for prayer that I wouldn't go insane. I had imposed enormous pressure on myself to be healed, or partly healed. When I wasn't healed the condemnation was overwhelming. I was sure my lack of progress was due to faithlessness or a wrong attitude on my part. I had been singled out in a crowd of sick people and told I would be healed. But I had failed, even when the odds were so high in my favour.

Helen tried to keep her thoughts to herself and encourage me. But her feelings of that time, so well hidden from me, are summed up in a letter she wrote to Mother:

> I would have given anything not to be the one to take Marg from that miracle service. Her face was twisted with such disappointment.
>
> I, myself, felt so disappointed. My heart ached for her. People's remarks didn't help. I was annoyed at their comments and insensitivity. We know the Lord's ways are not our ways, but I feel if they can't say anything edifying, it would be better to say nothing at all.

I feel angry when they try and impose their own ideas and stipulations on Marg.

From what I've witnessed in the services, God heals by instant supernatural power. There's no slow progress, just instantaneous results. That's how it will be for Marg, too!

The trauma had a spiral effect on those at home. My mother aged years under the emotional strain. After she had received the letter from Helen she took from under the bed a box full of photographs. There was the little girl she had coped with all those years. She had always been by my side when I needed her. But now she was miles across the world, needing her desperately, and she couldn't be there.

People often have trouble believing in healing, or believing they are healed. For me it was the opposite. Every fibre in my body had believed for at least a partial healing in that first miracle service. I fully expected to be healed and when I wasn't the blow was stunning. We didn't know what to do, what to believe for, whether to pack up and go home. We were almost scared to try again.

I questioned God endlessly. What did he mean when he told me I wouldn't come out of the chair until I had gone through such deep things I would never forget them. What deep things? Were they happening now? When would they finish? And what about the words 'I have chosen you'? Surely if God had chosen me he could heal me? When would I be healed? What was wrong with me? Why was the blasphemous arthritic healed and dedicated Christian Margie not? Was I possessed of the devil? Why hadn't my speech improved? Why didn't my body co-ordinate better?

At times I actually shook my fist into the face of God. Why, God? Why don't you answer? Why?

But I received no reply. It was mental, spiritual and emotional hell. All the 'confirmations' we had received before and during the service had turned to nothing. I couldn't even breathe any better.

During those weeks Helen was marvellous, trying to keep me constantly amused. We went shopping in the huge Los Angeles department stores day after day. When we weren't shopping we ate out or visited one of the many tourist attractions like Disneyland and Knott's Berry Farm.

But even in these fantasy worlds the reality of cerebral palsy wouldn't go away. We were sponsored through Disneyland by a Rotary Club, which also sent two girls to help Helen with me. It took three of them to get me on and off many of the activities, yet I still landed us in embarrassing situations. After we had seen the whale that swallowed Pinnochio I was mortified when I dropped my shoe in the drink, and Helen and the two Rotary girls spent ages trying to fish it out.

Amid all the confusion we did have times of great hilarity. We would spend hours looking in the boutiques with dresses like those Kathryn Kuhlman wore. Helen would hold them up against herself and then bend down and put them over me in my wheel-chair, while I lay back and dreamed of becoming Kathryn Kuhlman the second. Then Helen would take off Miss Kuhlman to a T. We collapsed into fits of laughter, completely oblivious to the disapproving looks of shop managers and other shoppers.

Yet every minute of every day I was searching desperately for the faintest sign of healing. I was still willing to grab hold of anything. I hadn't given up hope.

The closest I came to experiencing something tangible was when some nights, as I was about to fall asleep, I felt what seemed like an electric current passing through my brain. It was uncanny and more than a bit scary. Yet it was exciting. Surely this was it. But there was no physical demonstration of anything resulting from the currents. Just another false alarm, it seemed.

In our confusion we always tried to be positive, often

talking of what it would be like when I was healed. Out shopping, Helen would take down a pair of shoes, ones which my twisted feet could never wear, and say, 'Look at these, Marg. Aren't they fabulous? How about buying a pair of these when you are healed?'

Whenever we planned in advance to go somewhere I would say, 'Do you think I will walk by then?' Or sitting at lunch I would suddenly blurt out to Helen, 'What do you think the electric currents mean?'

People encouraged me that if my healing wasn't today it might be that night, or tomorrow, or a week later. The carrot of hope was always in front of me, but somehow I could never quite reach it.

Our conversation often turned to the first thing I would do when I was healed. Initially I thought of all the wonderful attractions in California that I couldn't enjoy from a wheelchair. How wonderful it would be to be free of all restrictions and go and do what I wanted. Perhaps I would go back to Disneyland and ride on the horse and carriage. But as I thought more, I knew I wanted something far more basic from life.

One day I looked over at Helen cutting up my doughnut so I could stab the pieces with a fork clutched clumsily between two hands. And suddenly I knew what I wanted to do when I was healed. Sure it would be great to run off to whatever tourist attraction I fancied. But all I really wanted was to pick up a doughnut in my fingers and put it in my mouth. Or to pick up a glass of juice in a lady-like manner. Or to do my buttons up, instead of sitting half-dressed until someone came and helped me. Or to dial the telephone. Or to type with my fingers so I could be employed, maybe as a secretary.

I wanted the use of my hands. Confinement in a wheelchair paled into insignificance when compared with the disadvantages presented by useless hands. Disneyland suddenly became irrelevant when compared with my inability to do the simple things in life.

So I clung to the hope that I would be healed. I waited for an explosion to take place in my brain; for God to reach down and set off the fire crackers which would make my hands and body function. At times I longed for it so hard that I ached.

Though Kathryn Kuhlman had left Los Angeles and was holding meetings in other parts of the country, we had the constant reminder of her powerful ministry through radio and television. Every morning I listened to her on the radio, and three mornings a week I watched her on television. Many people were healed just watching or listening in their living rooms. Every day I expected my healing right there and then.

I became very familiar with her ministry and methods through those television and radio programmes. She would interview Hollywood stars and prominent Christians and I would watch or listen, glued to her every word. As I took it all in, my mind would inevitably wander back to the Shrine, back to the beauty and splendour of Miss Kuhlman's miracle meetings themselves.

She hardly ever preached on healing itself. Her subjects included resisting temptation, faithfulness, the love of God, overcoming, alcoholism and End Times events. These messages barely lasted fifteen minutes. The rest of the time was taken up in songs, and testimonies of the good things God had done.

Her messages were short, simple and evangelistic. Sometimes they were unpredictable, as she would suddenly stop in mid-sentence, point her long index finger and whisper, 'He's here. The Holy Spirit is here. Reach out.'

Then the finger would point upwards, 'There's someone up in the balcony.' After that the finger would shoot off in another direction: 'Somebody in the wheelchair section, a spinal injury, a hip.' And the rows would come alive with people leaving their chairs and claiming healing.

The keys to her ministry were faith and love. She baptised her congregation with love. Tears rolled down her face as she saw the tremendous needs and reached out to help meet those needs. She would pray before speaking, 'All I have is my love. If you can use it, take it. I would die a thousand deaths before I would walk out on a platform. I know better than anyone else in the world that I have no healing virtue, no healing power. I depend on the power of the Holy Spirit.'

As she began to move around and speak, she would pause and say, 'The mighty Third Person is here. I feel like being seated, because he doesn't need me.'

She had a commanding, yet loving, presence on stage. She would stand motionless with her fingers raised and the choir behind her would sing, very quietly, 'Alleluia, alleluia.'

When a person was being healed she would encourage—'Walk across that stage, honey, walk across there.' And then she would laugh her short, high-pitched laugh, more a squeal of delight as the person responded.

She never laid hands on anyone before they were healed. She said she wanted to give all the glory to God, and prevent anyone thinking she had any power of her own.

Television also showed me the breadth of her ministry. On one programme she was interviewing Stan Mooneyham, of World Vision, who had just returned from a Vietnam hospital to which Miss Kuhlman had donated thousands of dollars. This had gone towards various child aids such as wheelchairs, little trolleys for spina bifidas, calipers and crutches.

'This is love,' she said as they were distributed, 'giving them what they need. Love talked about is easily pushed aside, but love demonstrated is irresistible.'

However, while this showed the extent of her

ministry, it confused me a little. Seeing her give wheel-chairs to disabled people at the same time as I was trying to believe myself out of mine was just a bit much.

Finally, after the ups and down of many weeks, Miss Kuhlman returned to Los Angeles and Helen and I prepared to attend our second, and last, Kathryn Kuhlman miracle service. Within days I would be winging my way back to New Zealand—healed or not.

My confidence had taken quite a battering in America, but I was determined not to let weakened faith rob me of the chance of physical freedom. I knew that hundreds of people back home were fasting and praying for me, pleading with God for my miracle.

It was at this second meeting that I had always believed I would see the totality of my healing. While at the first service, now a long month ago, I had fully expected some improvement, I had always believed that full restoration wouldn't occur until the second time I saw Miss Kuhlman in action. That would be the time when the vision of the beautiful preacher in the yellow dress would come to fruition.

I carefully donned my dress, and as it slipped over my shoulders I felt a new surge of faith and conviction. I had seen this dress in a vision from God. A young woman, dressed in yellow, with perfect movement, perfect co-ordination, perfect speech. The young woman had been me. I was dressed for my part. Now God would do his bit.

By the time we arrived at the Shrine, past dis-appointments were well behind me. I was certain that today I would be made whole. I was determined to step out and claim the vision.

This time I wouldn't allow my chair to have its red tag. Instead I asked to be removed from my chair so I could sit with the rest of the crowd. This was a step of faith, and my courage in doing so gave me a sense of freedom from the grip my chair seemed to have on my body. It gave the Lord the opportunity to prove himself, to prove his power. I wasn't going to limit him, nor did I wish to hinder my healing any further. If I took the first step, the Lord would meet me with the second, I thought.

The meeting was almost identical to the first one. The only difference was the audience. Different people were being healed.

I closed my eyes and worshipped God during the singing, enjoying his presence. People nearby reached out and touched me, praying for me in love and expecting a miracle with me. 'Today, today it's your turn. It must be today,' they said, smiling in assurance.

As before, miracle after miracle began to occur— cancer, Parkinson's disease, multiple sclerosis. The deaf heard, the blind saw, the lame walked. I waited, and before long noticed to my alarm that cerebral palsy was never among the ailments. Every condition, it seemed, could be cured, except cerebral palsy.

'With God all things are possible,' I recited under my breath, battling to overcome that jolt to my faith. But I knew I had to see cerebral palsy healed before I could really believe it.

Then, right before my eyes, it happened. An eleven-year-old boy named Craig staggered on to the stage. A cerebral palsy sufferer. Apparently he had been partly healed during the service, but he still walked with spastic gait as he swayed across the platform.

I looked at this little boy and thought, 'Well, if that's a healing, God, forget it. You're either healed or you're not. I don't want this half way business. When Jesus heals, he heals completely.'

But the miracle hadn't finished, it had only just begun. Miss Kuhlman called to him, 'Come on, honey. Stand tall, straight like a soldier. Make those little legs go. Ride a bike. Make those legs ride a bike. Copy me.'

The boy lifted his legs, and began wheeling them in the motion of riding a bike. Then, suddenly, he took off and ran right pass Miss Kuhlman and around the choir. She started following, chasing him around the stage, and the crowd erupted at this amazing scene of God at work. Craig was grinning from ear to ear. Suddenly the cerebral palsy awkwardness was gone. He moved with perfect co-ordination and timing. This was it! Cerebral palsy, quite literally, was on the run. This was my time to reach out, the time I had been waiting for! An American friend leaned over, 'Marg, it's got to be you next, it must be you.'

I slowly rose to my feet, stretching, waiting for my legs to strengthen and hold my body for the first time in my life. I reached out to God, expectant. This was the time—cerebral palsy healing time.

'Stand up,' I said to myself. I jerked upright and strained towards the ceiling of that heavenly Shrine, desperate that my legs would respond. And as I rose, my faith surged to a new peak, sure that if God could heal Craig, he could certainly heal me. Ten thousand miles for a miracle, and here was the miracle. I would stand tall, I would walk, run, skip and dance. I would do all those normal things like dressing myself and cutting up my own food. This was my moment of discovery.

My legs ached and wobbled, but my determination didn't wane one bit. Just a few seconds more, hold on, Marg, it's about to happen now.

And then it happened. With a crash that seemed to echo throughout that massive auditorium, I collapsed back into my seat, quivering and overwhelmed with exhaustion and crushing disappointment. The conditions had been so right—cerebral palsy was being healed—and there I was slumped in my chair. But still my hope burned. If only I could be prayed for personally by Kathryn Kuhlman.

The ushers found my wheelchair and wheeled me down to the side entrance of the Shrine. A big crowd was congregating and the only place they could find for me was behind the stage doors. Around me people were screaming, 'I'm healed!' Tears of joy were running down their faces. I was happy for them, and really excited for little Craig. But I was bitterly disappointed for myself. And I was angry with God. He had failed me at the crucial moment. He had made me a laughing stock. Why, God, why?

I was also angry with Kathryn Kuhlman, prancing off the stage and not worrying about the ruin and disappointment she left behind.

After about twenty minutes Miss Kuhlman appeared, spoke briefly to me, then took my face in her hands as she began to say, 'Precious Jesus, precious Jesus.'

I looked up into her face and was shocked to see what a mess it was. And I realised I had been wrong. She *did* care. Her make-up had run from crying so much, revealing the immense emotional conflict she imposed on herself in order to see so many healed.

'Precious Jesus,' she repeated. I felt a blackness descend on me, as if I was fainting. But slowly a crack appeared in the blackness, like a light being turned on, and I was very briefly bathed in light. I could feel the presence of God, just momentarily.

Then, just as quickly, it was gone. As I came around, Miss Kuhlman was walking away. I wasn't healed and I wasn't going to be healed. Nothing worked, not even a touch from Kathryn Kuhlman herself.

I watched her walk to her car, and as she went she was mobbed by the crowd, her clothes virtually torn from her body. I was appalled, even through my bitter disappointment. I felt ashamed, not so much for their actions, but for the fact that I would have done the same if I had been able to walk.

Two days later we were to fly back to New Zealand, and during that time I struggled with the desire to live at all. I didn't want to go home. I didn't even want to ring my parents who were expecting me to announce I was healed. I was returning to more unemployment and more frustration at having a bright mind inside a disobedient body. I had nothing.

The last straw came just hours before we were due to fly home. Helen was struggling to manoeuvre my wheelchair over the kerb when a man suddenly came out of nowhere and said to her, 'Why don't you shoot the bastard and forget you ever had her?'

The words were bad enough, but was was worse was that in a way he had a point.

Yet I also knew he was wrong. Despite my disenchantment with God, deep down inside I knew he was still real. And he didn't lie. If I didn't believe God, I would have asked that man for a gun and pulled the trigger myself. But I knew God would come up with the answers. He'd better.

8

Picking up the Pieces

The jet's engines whined incessantly as I returned to
New Zealand, each passing minute taking me a few
miles further from the scene of my shattered dreams.
But my emotional and spiritual wounds were still raw.
It would be a long time, if ever, before I could get over
the events of the previous seven weeks.

What hurt the most, as I dully pondered my
American nightmare, was the callous statement from
one spiritual know-all as I was wheeled out of the
Shrine's swinging doors for the last time.

'Don't worry,' he promised, 'your healing will come.
It's lack of faith, you see. It's only those who truly
believe...Jesus never failed to heal any who came to
him.'

And off he walked, content that he had done his
duty for God, but blissfully unaware that he was
actually piling destruction onto devastation.

Doubts, fears and depression threatened to overwhelm me as the plane's engines continued to roar
away. I wanted to scream, to cry, maybe to die. What
would my family say? What would my friends say? I
thought of the two elders who had discussed my
condition before I left. The pessimistic one was right.
What future did I have now?

The aircraft bumped as it hit turbulence. Writhing
within, I grappled with a sense of condemnation. I

thought of all those who had sacrificed huge amounts of money to make my pilgrimage possible. It frustrated me to think I had failed them. Yet deep within, I still toyed with the idea that maybe God was just delaying my deliverance. I longed to walk from that plane to my family when it finally arrived at Auckland Airport. I still had a wild and fantastic hope. Fantasy seemed far preferable to the reality of life in a wheelchair.

When Molly and I had left Auckland Airport just seven short weeks previously, we were given a rousing and enthusiastic send-off by dozens of friends and well-wishers who wanted to be a part of the miracle that was about to happen. Laughter punctuated our conversations in the knowledge that the beginning of the end was upon us.

Yet those seven short weeks could have been seven long years, so different was the reception on my return. No fanfare, no excitement. And, worst of all, no people. Of the dozens who turned out to see me off, only my family and two close friends were there when I returned.

I was crushed. When I really needed my friends—when I desperately wanted someone to say it didn't matter, that they loved me anyway—I was abandoned. Yet I didn't blame them. Instead I blamed God.

I knew life would never be the same. But adjusting to New Zealand again was harder than I had thought. Kathy Bowen had flown the nest and I felt an acute lack of true, close friends. My time in America had been full and lively. I'd been to Disneyland, Knott's Berry Farm and Hollywood Universal Studios. I'd shopped wherever and whenever I could. I'd not only attended the Kathryn Kuhlman services at the Shrine, but any healing service in the greater Los Angeles area. Everything had been on a larger scale—the pace faster, the lights brighter, the entertainment jazzier. Coming back to my own four walls was like being sentenced to solitary confinement. I was now mature enough to accept this, so I wasn't bitter. But I felt dreadfully alone, very conscious of a void in my life. However, as always, God had my need for a close friend and confidant in hand. Even as Kathy left, another even more fulfilling friendship was developing.

Though I had known Hugh and Di Willis for many years, it was only after returning from America that I came to rely on their support and loyalty. Di, a trained occupational therapist, was small in stature with dark curly hair, vibrant eyes and a vivacious personality. Yet she possessed a deep sensitivity and compassion, and a gift for understanding the emotions and frustrations of the disabled seldom found in an able-bodied person. Her exuberance was a tonic to me. It was impossible to remain morose around her for long.

Tall, lanky Hugh was Di's opposite—studious, quiet and reserved. A man of few words, his gentle blue eyes often communicated for him. Together they made a great team—both needing the other's qualities to complete their own. So great was their love and commitment for the disabled that they had built a house in Auckland specially designed to cater for the needs of their wheelchair-bound friends.

My relationship with Di developed through correspondence and through regular holiday visits to their home. Very soon Di and I became like sisters. We looked alike, our names were alike (Willis and Willers) and she was just four years older than I. So I called her 'Big Sis'.

Di devoted hours to me when I returned from America, ensuring I was kept happy and stimulated by a whirl of social activity. She understood what I had been through overseas, and showed tremendous sensitivity in helping me cope. It was she who launched me into a public role for the first time, arranging a forty-five guest dinner party at the home of one of her former patients, a quadriplegic. I was to be the guest speaker. The meeting was a stunning success with people seeming to hang on to my every word. Before I knew it I was involved with a succession of women's meetings. Di led the way and I frantically hung on to her coat-tails, trying to describe this miracle and that miracle, this situation and that scene from the Kathryn Kuhlman healing services—all to women who listened in fascination, unaware that such miracles were occurring in their twentieth-century world.

I told the stories with vibrancy, and crowds responded with amazement. Disabled people began to enquire about the possibility of them going to be healed at a Kathryn Kuhlman meeting. Some even made plans to make the big trip to America—perhaps it would be 10,000 miles for their miracle too. I was always enthusiastic when they asked me, and encouraged them to stretch out and believe. But I could never bring myself to share the broken heart which I was carrying inside.

The meetings were exhilarating. I was getting the chance to speak as I had always dreamed. I could hardly believe the way my shaky and sometimes barely intelligible voice could hold the attention of a crowd. But every miracle I enthusiastically related to the gatherings seemed to turn the knife of disappointment inside me. My hypocritical life was crumbling and these meetings were contributing to it. I felt as delicate as a piece of porcelain. The speaking engagements, the small-scale fame and respect, were merely papering over major cracks. Sooner or later, I knew, I would fall apart.

Many people at the meetings overlooked my own lack of healing. Others whispered behind backs and hands, wondering why there was no improvement in my body. Older women came up, in church or on the street, clucked their tongues and said, 'Oh, you poor dear brave, brave girl,' or, 'Perhaps now you'll come to your senses and accept your handicap.' Others posed heavy spiritual answers or dogmatic theories as to why I hadn't been healed. I maintained a brave face throughout it all, smiling politely to hide feelings which were often far from charming.

The Jesus 75 crusade was the talk of the city at that time, and one night I joined thousands of others in going to hear a dynamic American evangelist who had a reputed gift of healing—Ray Mossholder. Unknown to me, however, my escorts for the night were very healing-orientated. Sure enough, when the invitation was given they gripped the handles of my wheelchair and pushed me to the healing room, despite my strong protestations. Whether I wanted it or not I was going to be prayed for. My healing would be tonight! At least that's what they said. I wasn't consulted, and neither was God.

Hot tears spilled down my cheeks. This was too much. Entering the healing room, I was conscious of the excitement and anticipation around me. I saw a woman kneeling in prayer, and before my eyes an apple-sized lump on the back of her neck withered and disappeared. Spontaneous dancing and rejoicing followed. All I could do was suppress the dread of the moment. I wasn't in the room by choice. Flashbacks of the Shrine services entombed me. I felt trapped.

Slowly Ray Mossholder approached me. His sensitive eyes looked into mine as I briefly explained my disability and my experiences at the great Kathryn Kuhlman services. He was understanding, gentle and loving, and seemed to be inwardly communing with the Holy Spirit's instruction. He moved on to pray for others, leaving me for a while. Beside me was a hunch-backed man who smelled strongly of dirt and sweat. He was in his fifties, but he looked closer to ninety. As Ray Mossholder reached down to him in compassion, the man began to weep. 'Jesus, Jesus, Jesus,' he whispered over and over again. 'Thank you, Jesus. Oh, thank you, Jesus.' Then his body straightened, and like

a sprinter out of the starting block he was on his
feet. More joy, more euphoria. God was moving in
power!

Across the room I noticed my friend Joe, who also
had cerebral palsy. He was prancing delightedly, but
still with his cerebral palsy gait, beside himself with joy.
His cerebral palsy seemed to have improved. It didn't
matter that there wasn't a total healing—just as long
as there was some form of improvement.

Ray Mossholder responded enthusiastically. 'You do
very well for a cerebral palsy man.' His words were
drowned as the crowd erupted in applause. Joe
beamed.

After praying for several others, Ray Mossholder
was unexpectedly beside my chair. 'Oh my God, what
now?' I thought wearily. But his soothing voice calmed
me as his hand caressed my cheek.

'Honey,' he began, 'don't worry about the bitterness.
Jesus understands. It's only human to have these
feelings. God doesn't condemn us for our natural
feelings, though it's important what we do with them. I
sense you're a woman of tremendous calibre and
character. The time will come when you can invite the
Lord into these painful turning points in your life.
This suffering will not be wasted, but will be for the
glory of God.'

I don't remember him actually praying for me, just
the sensation of his hands resting lightly on my head. I
opened my eyes and he was gone, so quickly, walking
across the floor to pray for someone else. I was
unchanged, unhealed.

I appreciated his warm words, but words weren't
enough. I returned home on an emotional downer. I
began to react to situations more like an angry
dog than a human being. Even my great visions and
wonderful encounters with God over the years weren't
enough to see me through. I had been badly battered,
and my faith was at an all-time low. I could barely trust

God any more, let alone believe in his power. I was sucked down into a bottomless pit of self-pity.

Alone in my room, hour after hour, I grappled with God, as I knelt at my bed, my prayers growing louder and louder as my frustration with God increased. *'Faith arise. Heal me, God,'* I cried out in exasperation. 'Father, increase my faith. Lord Jesus, increase my faith.' And as a final demand, I exploded: *'Heal me! I hate being a hopeless bum.'* Then I tried another tack. Perhaps I was taking God for granted. So I asked for forgiveness and for a cleansed and purified life. I confessed all my sins, real or imagined, past, present and future, any hang-ups, worries and woes. And I waited. 'Lord, that I might be whole. That I might declare the wonderful works of God.' But the room was like a lead-lined box, the prayers bounced uselessly around my room, echoing back at me.

At one point I wondered if I was praying to the wrong person. *'Holy Spirit!'* I screamed instead. 'It's Margie. You know, down here in TePuke, where the kiwi fruit grow. I'm waiting to be healed. Come, Holy Spirit. Let me receive your healing power. My mouth is wide open and ready to receive.'

My body was tense with expectancy. I almost lifted off the floor in my readiness to run, leap and praise God.

Nothing. Absolutely nothing. The floor grew hard. My knees hurt. It may have been five minutes, or it may have been fifteen. Eventually I rose slowly and sobbing hysterically threw myself across the bed. At that point my sister Helen burst in, unable to bear my agony any longer without intervening.

'Marg, stop it! *Stop it!*' she shouted, reaching down to pull me up.

'I'm not one of them,' I hissed at her.

'One of what?'

'God's favourites!' I shrieked. 'Leave me alone. Just get out of here!'

'Pull yourself together,' she commanded. 'Avoiding reality isn't going to help. You've got to face the truth. You are not going to be healed—not at this time.'

'Stop griping about what you don't have,' Helen went on determinedly. 'Stop ranting and raving like a lunatic. Learn to make the most of life. Get to grips with yourself. The whole neighbourhood can hear you.'

'Get out of here!' I yelled in return. 'You don't understand. I've had a bellyful of everyone. Nobody understands. Not you, not Mum and Dad, not friends or pastors. Not even God!' Even as I spoke, I was disgusted with myself.

This ebb and flow of emotions continued for several months. Frustrations built up within me and I'd erupt like a demanding child, yelling at God and others to demand attention.

'For goodness sake, Margie,' Di exclaimed one day. 'You're always beautifully dressed. You've got a pretty face, and more. Your life offers so much hope to others, but you've let yourself go. You've got such potential in the hands of God! Stop being hung up on self-image. Stop putting yourself down. Stop being so defensive.'

Her down-to-earth advice was right, but it was irritating to me. If the truth be known, I didn't want to stop.

Di continued, speaking to me over her shoulder as she mixed a cake. She explained that society determined our values, and that we always come out the loser when we evaluate ourselves according to someone else's ideas and standards. 'A sportsman measures you by your athletic ability,' she said. 'A student measures you by your brain. A boyfriend or girlfriend by your good looks. And it's always a losing battle. We have to forget what people say and think and stop competing according to the world's rules. It's God's values that are the important ones.'

She was right, of course. God knew I had arms, legs, feet and hands that didn't co-operate with the trunk of my body, but he had made me—he had allowed it to happen. He wasn't embarrassed about my disability. Why should I be?

Di encouraged me to reach out anew, allowing God's love to lift me into new discoveries of all the good things he had planned for my life. She urged me to pray, 'Lord, what can you do with me?' rather than say 'I can't, I'm useless.'

From that day on, I began to let go of my anger and resentment.. Many barriers I had thrown up myself had to be broken. Gradually, my self-image improved. I knew that as long as I sought to hide my problems, there would be no release within. The devil loves to work in the dark, but exposing things to the light breaks the power of darkness.

At least this was the case until I attended an outdoor meeting in November. During the evening someone, who claimed they didn't know my situation, boomed forth a word of prophecy. 'There was healing tonight for a lady who has travelled 10,000 miles for a miracle,' he declared. I looked around. My stomach sank. The message was obviously directed at me. Suddenly, I was whisked indoors for yet another intense healing session.

Three of us pranced around the lounge for three hours—from 10 pm until 1 am—praying, praising and commanding healing to come. My muscles became torn and stretched, my body screamed for respite. Yet I forced myself on. My companions blurred as I resolutely tried to reach out for the promised healing. But it all ended in the same way as it had umpteen times before. I collapsed, exhausted and unhealed.

I searched furiously, frantically, for the key. So many accusations were being thrown at me: 'Don't think the girl really wants to be healed...lack of faith ...sins visited from the forefathers...maybe her great-grandfather shot Abraham Lincoln. ...'

Preposterous as many of them were, I was becoming unable to discern right from wrong, fact from fiction, wisdom from foolishness.

Once again, bitterness festered in my subconscious. I couldn't ignore the root of my trouble, or repress my anger towards God. I tried hard, but it was like plastering over a boil. The poison spread unseen throughout me, emerging in bouts of moodiness and violent outrage.

So, worn down by inner conflict and guilt, I sought help from Sister Joy Smith. A former missionary, Sister Joy was a member of the pastoral staff at a large church in Auckland. She was a woman of wisdom and authority in spiritual gifts and I had come to respect and trust her through hearing her preach and seeing her minister. Di made an appointment for me to see her and took me to the counselling centre.

I was wheeled in, my chair secured and Di discreetly made her exit. I sat there, nervous and alone. I tried to collect my thoughts, and began to wish I'd never agreed to come. But it was too late.

The door suddenly opened and a charge of dynamite swept the room. Petite, gry-haired, a veritable ball of explosive energy, she resembled the rushing wind of Pentecost. Sister Joy greeted me briefly and then launched straight into prayer. I watched her surreptitiously as she paced back and forth across the room. Head up, head down, arms up in the air, arms clasped behind her then in front, she was totally absorbed in conversation with God, doing business with him on my behalf. I was intrigued by her vitality and the startling reality of her conversation with the Father.

Every so often she'd whirl towards me to ask a question, then just as quickly return to her pacing and praying.

'Have you forgiven the doctor who was responsible for the mismanagement at your birth?' she asked.

'I've never held a grudge against the man,' I replied honestly. 'Never.'

'Were you a wanted baby, loved? Were you accepted by your parents?'

There followed a torrent of questions, many of which related to my childhood, interspersed always with periods of prayer.

Sister Joy was a woman of intense spirituality. She was extremely sensitive, despite the boundless energy which took me aback at times. Even though she had never married, she was deeply maternal. A trained midwife, she was obviously used to babies—both natural and spiritual.

Despite all her qualities, however, I realised that she was powerless to resolve my inner conflict and turmoil unless I was willing to be helped. I was at a crossroads. Would I let go and let God control my life again? Sister Joy encouraged me to open up and expose my hidden feelings—my disappointments and failures, my long-ings and fears. Her sensitivity and magnetic love were so wonderful that I began to respond. Slowly at first, but then with increasing openness and honesty, I poured out my heart.

'The lights have gone out,' I confessed. 'I don't experience any joy or happiness. At times I've even lost the will to live. There's no purpose to life. I'm swallowed up in complete darkness. God has abandoned me! My prayer life has stagnated. My words don't go any further than the ceiling. I've known exciting times with God, received visions and experienced supernatural encounters. But now it's as if the Holy Spirit has left me.'

And then, the key moment that Sister Joy—and God—knew had to come from me: 'Something is wrong, very wrong! Help me! I've confessed every sin I know,' I sobbed. 'I've pushed all the buttons, pulled all the levers. I've done all I've been asked to do. But nothing works. Nothing! I ask for this, believe God for that, and the opposite happens.'

Sister Joy reached for my hand. 'Keep praying,' she counselled. 'Keep reaching out and moving in to God. Margie,' she continued, her voice soft, 'every Christian experiences periods of darkness. Just remember, whatever the problem, God has allowed this to happen.' She looked directly at me. 'Do you know, you can be going through one of the greatest trials ever faced and still be in the perfect will of God? I believe that America and all that has been inflicted on you has been both appointed and approved by God. God is in complete control of the situation, not the devil.'

'You don't think I'm possessed by the devil, then?' I blurted out.

Sister Joy shook her head. 'God is in control,' she reaffirmed.

'Do you think God created disability, then?' I asked, somewhat defiantly.

She reached for her Bible and thumbed through the well-worn pages to Exodus 4:11, where Moses questions God about his lack of eloquence. God's response was: 'Who gave man his mouth? Who makes him deaf or dumb? Who gives him sight or makes him blind? Is it not I, the Lord?'

I gulped and stared at Sister Joy. I had never seen the scriptures like that before. She turned to Psalm 139 and read out the passage about God being present when I was formed in utter seclusion; how he saw me before I was born and arranged each day of my life before I even breathed.

'Margie,' she said keenly, 'if God was present while you were being formed in your mother's womb, he was certainly present at your birth.'

I hesitated, then blurted out a question that had always haunted me: 'What about the sins of the forefathers being visited on this generation?'

Sister Joy again quickly flicked through the pages of her Bible, stopping at John's account of the blind man healed, where Jesus said that not all physical problems are due to personal or parental sin.

'God has placed his hand on you in a marvellous and wonderful way, Margie,' she said. 'God's not going to let you go. When he takes us through testings, fires and suffering, he may take us right to boiling point. But he will not take us beyond what we can endure.' She leapt to her feet and recited:

> 'Those He trusts, He tests with fire
> To strengthen and complete
> And those who have the greatest worth
> must bear the greatest heat!'

Pulling a handkerchief from her pocket, she blew her nose loudly.

'Sometimes,' she whispered, choked, 'it can take more faith to remain in a wheelchair and want to keep living than it does to rise up and walk.'

Tears streamed down my face. I realised that healing of the soul was far more important than healing of the body. Sister Joy was far more concerned with the inner me—and she was right!

'Let's pray,' she invited, once again in control of her emotions. 'When we are left with shattered plans, I know God has far better plans.'

I didn't respond. Maybe some day I could accept God's better plans—but not yet.

Sister Joy didn't seem to notice my lack of response. Like a bolt from the blue she said, 'Let's express to God how much we love him. Let's thank him for this wheelchair, and the blessing it is...'

'What!' I shrieked, interrupting her in mid-sentence. I was slowly coming to terms with not being healed, but to see my chair as a blessing was beyond reasoning. 'You're nuts!' I raged. 'No, I won't! If you want to express thanks to God, go right ahead, but don't expect me to!'

It was as if a plaster over a festering boil had been

torn aside, exposing the poison beneath. I felt—and acted—like garbage.

'Margie,' Sister Joy said steadily. 'God loves you so much.'

'I'm in hell!' I spat back. 'Life in a chair is living hell! I would rather be dead!' Then I added, 'But you wouldn't know about that, would you?'

Sister Joy was on her feet again, dancing as she praised God and prayed for me. I seethed inwardly. The audacity of the woman, dancing before my chair! Just let her move closer, I thought. And as she did I lashed out with my fist, skimming the top of her nose.

'God's a liar!' I screamed, shocked with myself, yet somehow exultant. 'He promised to heal me. How can I trust God? My dreams are shattered! I'm at a dead end! I had a vision...I was tall and straight...I preached like a man ..' My voice trailed into a wail.

Sister Joy didn't even blink. 'A snap of God's fingers and that vision could become a reality,' she retorted. 'But often the miracle God awaits is not physical but spiritual—it's that of a surrendered life. That, Margie, takes time! Vision comes from God, but often God doesn't bring it to birth immediately. It may take years to come to fruition, but in his time he makes all things beautiful. He watches over his vision; he is faithful about bringing it to reality. He is a God of integrity. God is not a man that he should lie.'

Tears of rage, brokenness and desolation streamed down my cheeks.

'God is going to make you like Job,' Sister Joy went on, 'a man tried as gold.'

'I'm not Job!' I shrieked.

'God must conquer the man or woman he trusts with his great will and plan.' It was as if Sister Joy hadn't heard my outburst. 'God can't trust some people with toothache, but he trusts you with your chair and your disabilities. God has a plan for your life, Margie. Plans for good and not for evil, to give you a future and a hope.' She eyed me squarely from across the room. Her voice was husky again. 'Jesus loves you, Margie. He loves you.'

'How very spiritual,' I responded sarcastically.

Seconds ticked by. For once she seemed lost for words. Moistening her lips, she spoke the one thing I wasn't prepared for—and couldn't handle. 'He does love you—and so do I.'

It was like a knock-out punch in a boxing match. I stared back glassy-eyed from the canvas. Nobody could love me after the way I had just behaved. Yet Sister Joy did. I didn't need to believe her words, I could see it in her eyes.

My defiance crumpled. I couldn't fight love such as that. Love removes all obstacles. Love broke me down.

She came across the room and took me in her arms.

'Let's pray together,' she said. 'Let's release it all to Jesus. Let's not go hankering after what is not in his timing.'

I tried to respond, but my crying only increased. As she prayed, her arms around me, I could barely make out her words over my sobs.

'You are acting for our highest good,' she prayed. 'When you answer no to our prayers, we accept your no, Father. And I believe you will turn these scars into stars.'

I still struggled within. Emotionally, I still didn't want to give thanks—not yet. But I could, and would, express my love to God with my will—even if I couldn't with my feelings.

Slowly, hesitantly, I bowed my head, if not my heart, and thanked God for my chair.

9

Faith Bible College

There is a saying, 'Hope is not discouraged by the past, but believes in the promises of the future.' Hesitantly, like a slowly opening flower, I again began to reach out to God, trying to discover who I was and what I could become. I had overcome one hurdle in thanking God for my chair. But I still had to deal with the remaining inner hurt and hot anger. It didn't come easily. But slowly, ever so slowly, I shed the bitterness and hostility which had their roots in my American nightmare.

'Lord,' I prayed. 'I want your will. I give myself to you exactly as I am. What can you do with me?'

One little verse, Jeremiah 33:3, tumbled over and over in my mind: 'Call to me and I will answer you and tell you great and unsearchable things you do not know.'

At first I couldn't see its relevance. And yet it was always nagging at the back of my mind, coming to the fore at the most unusual times. Little did I realise that this verse was God's gentle way of directing me into the next step in my life's odyssey—Bible college.

I had first visited Faith Bible College two years earlier, and had become a regular visitor for week-long schools each spring and autumn. The college, a short-term missionary training centre, is nestled between rolling hills on the outskirts of Tauranga. It is surrounded by wooded and landscaped grounds from

108

which one can enjoy panoramic views. This tranquil atmosphere encouraged one to appreciate both creation and the Creator.

Twice a year open schools were held often coinciding with the visit of a well-known overseas lecturer. Open invitations were extended to the public to join the student body.

Men and women of tremendous calibre and freshness of faith had addressed those schools—people like Derek Prince, Brian Bailey and Bob Mumford from overseas, and a host of well-known preachers throughout New Zealand. I was inspired and challenged by such a wide cross-section of teachers, covering a broad spectrum of subjects.

Bob Mumford was probably my favourite. He was an amazing communicator with a tremendous sense of humour. He had taught retarded children, and realised that to share the love of God with them he had to find a method to make them understand. So he used body language, accentuating everything he said with gestures. Years later this style was still evident as he taught the students at Faith. He stood on chairs, paced the aisle and used all kinds of actions to imprint the lesson on the students' minds. 'A merry heart doeth good like a medicine,' the Bible says, and it was not hard to have a 'merry heart' when Bob was teaching. There were times when I laughed so hard I was quite uncontrollable. And as I laughed, healing took place within; an inner healing caused by my merriness of heart.

There were many different moods in the classroom at Faith—not just times of hilarity. We spent long periods at the beginning and end of every lecture in praise and prayer, and many times we spontaneously burst into song during the lectures themselves.

At other times even singing praises seemed inappropriate. Those were times of awesome silence as the presence of God enfolded us. All through these wonderful experiences, that little verse, Jeremiah 33:3, continued to impress itself upon me.

Eventually the message came through loud and clear. God had already spoken to me about training for ministry, but now I sensed he was calling me to Bible college—to step out in faith to 'Faith'. The doubts lingered. Bible college was an awesome challenge from a wheelchair.

'Why do you want to go to Bible college?' Di asked me, as I shared my thoughts with her.

'My goal is to prepare myself for useful Christian service,' I explained. 'And I must confess I'm hankering to return to the States. I would love to go to more miracle services at the Shrine Auditorium.' I was still corresponding with Kathryn Kuhlman, despite my traumatic experiences at her meetings.

Di's eyebrows shot up and a sigh escaped her lips. 'You're a tiger for punishment,' she said. 'If I'd been through what you went through in America, there's no way you'd get me near that place again!'

'Well then,' I hesitated, searching for the right words, 'I suggest you've never wanted anything badly enough. If you did, you'd be prepared to endure anything!'

I was still a mixed-up kid with mixed-up goals, mixed-up emotions and no clear direction for my life. And I was still frustrated by condemning thoughts of having failed to be healed. Deep down I still believed that God wanted me to stand on my feet, and when I could stand physically, all the blanks in my life would naturally fall into place.

Di sensed my inner conflict. 'Failure isn't final with God,' she said kindly. 'Just because you're not healed, it doesn't mean you're a failure. Look, if you're going to try new things, you're always going to experience some kind of failure. I am convinced that God is more pleased with those who step out in faith and fail than with those who sit back and do nothing for fear of failure.

God can turn our mistakes around and bring good out of what appears to be disaster,' Di went on. 'It's crucial that we learn to handle failure positively if we are to deepen our relationship with God. Remember the stories of Peter, David, Moses and all those other heroes of our faith? They had faith to risk failure. Don't let failure make you scared when reaching out to God,' she urged. 'Allow him to turn your trials into triumphs, your stumbling blocks to stepping stones, your tests to testimonies. Remember, God has chosen you for an appointed task. He doesn't lie. I believe that promise you were given will be fulfilled.

'Margie, if God is speaking to you about Faith Bible College, then trust him—step out and make your application. Be like the priests before the Red Sea and step into the waters allowing God to do the parting.'

I was aware that I would encounter difficulties, even opposition, if I went to Bible college. The buildings weren't designed for wheelchairs; I would need assistance at meal times; though I could almost dress myself, I needed help with buttons, zips, hooks-and-eyes; and I wouldn't be able to use my typewriter in the classroom because of the disruption to recording the lectures.

All these hurdles, and countless others, loomed large. But despite the obstacles, I was by now constantly talking, thinking and dreaming Faith Bible College.

Eventually, pushing aside the fears, I wrote to the registrar, requesting an interview for a place on the next eighteen-week standard training course. Kaye Hurn, the women's dean, well remembers receiving my letter. She realised with a sinking feeling that it was from 'that woman' she had seen in the distance during the autumn and spring schools. She had always been careful to avoid me when the meeting was over, considering me as totally handicapped—physically and mentally.

But she was about to be surprised. After a suitable time had been arranged, Kaye travelled to our home for the 'dreaded interview'.

Before knocking on the front door, she breathed a silent prayer, asking God for wisdom, for a release of his love. Then taking a deep breath she opened the door and stepped inside.

'I'm not mentally retarded, you know,' I blurted out as Kaye walked through to the living room. 'I'm only physically handicapped.'

Relief spread across her face as she realised she was about to interview someone who was actually quite intelligent. As we talked she was able to forget my physical limitations.

'I began to see a young woman with the call of God on her life, and a desire to prepare herself the best way she could for whatever lay ahead,' she wrote later. 'My natural mind thought of all the reasons why we couldn't have her as a student, but my spirit was excited. I understood the Lord wanted her at college as a student, and he would see to every detail.'

Kaye's report was positive, but the final decision on my application lay with the college board. They were well aware of the difficulties that would occur if they accepted me as a full-time student. So they committed my application to earnest prayer. As they prayed, God clearly indicated they were to accept me. God had parted the Red Sea for me, again giving me a clear sign of his purposes for my life. This time his purpose was for me to sit at his feet and learn. The clarity of my acceptance became the anchor that held me through the times of questioning and difficulties that were to follow.

It was February, 1976. Excitement and nervousness bubbled to the surface, but deep down I felt a peace— the peace of God that I was doing the right thing! The packing and the goodbyes were over, the promises of prayer support and letter-writing had been made. I'd been anticipating this day all summer. After weeks of preparation and prayer I was on my way to Faith Bible College.

My mind raced as we drove through the gates, down the short windy drive and into the college campus. What lay ahead? What would my room be like? How would I cope with lectures and assignments? Would I pass or fail? Was I really going to grow and mature? How would I learn to live and interact with seventy strangers who probably knew nothing about disability —let alone cerebral palsy?

There was so much to learn—what do do, how to do it! I wanted to excel, to be understood and above all to be accepted. The answer to every question was the same. I didn't know, but God did.

As we stopped in the carpark, I muttered a thankful prayer. Ramps had been installed at the lecture rooms, dining rooms and also the dormitory block. One major hurdle overcome.

We were shown to my room and left to unpack. It was adequate, if a little small and drably furnished. A hush descended as we began to bring out my clothes, books and special treasures from home. My mother began to make my room look as homely as possible— frilly pillow slips, a mobile of fluffy, pale-pink swans on the ceiling and a deep-pink bed cover. Within a very few minutes the room had become familiar, comfortable and feminine.

Mother helped me into my dinner gown for the evening's candle-lit dinner to celebrate the beginning of a very special adventure in Faith. And then, amid hugs and kisses, she was gone. I was now on my own.

I propelled my way to the dining hall. All the guys and girls presented themselves, each with a touch of shyness, showered, polished and thoroughly laundered. Ready for anything. As I looked around at the scores of enthusiastic faces my excitement mounted. How wonderful to be with so many people hungry for the word of God, and desiring to know and obey his perfect will.

I relaxed a little at this realisation, but my tension returned after dinner when students were asked to introduce themselves and say briefly why they had come to Faith. Though I am not shy, the thought of speaking before the whole college board and faculty, plus fifty-three fellow students, suddenly terrified me.

By the time my turn came, my tongue struggled to form words and my face flushed. I lifted my gaze to the back of the room, riveting my eyes on a knot of wood in the back wall. And as I wrestled with my words, the full severity of my disability hit home—both to myself and to everyone else in the room.

Some were embarrassed and looked down at the floor. Others were angry. 'What in the world is she doing here?' someone hissed. 'What demented person let her into the college?' And the more I panicked, the more my voice deteriorated.

But as I floundered on I sensed a change of atmosphere. The stark reality of my circumstances drew their compassion. Several had listened hard and deciphered my words. They responded to my obvious effort with nods and soft 'amens'. The hostility disappeared as quickly as it had arisen, and was replaced with overwhelming waves of loving support. My two-minute eternity finally ended. I sat trembling but pleased. Another hurdle overcome.

Principal Des Short concluded by explaining how God had given a 'clear green light' for me to be accepted as part of the student body. And at his invitation I was encouraged to address the students the next morning about how to relate to the disabled.

The evening concluded with a time when everyone praised and worshipped the One who had led them there. I returned to my room exhausted. I hadn't the energy, or the nerve, to venture out to the bathroom. Breathing a silent prayer of thanks for the quality of my bladder, I managed to slip off my clothes and slide between the sheets. In the morning I would need someone to help me dress, but that was tomorrow and I resolved to let that care for itself.

Sleep eluded me, however. I was increasingly aware that my struggles weren't over. In fact they were just beginning. Suddenly I felt very alone and afraid, in a strange room and a strange bed, hearing strange noises. My anxieties mounted. What if I couldn't cope? What about the barriers still to be overcome?

I felt the frustration of being physically dependent upon others who didn't necessarily have any under-standing or natural insight about how to assist me in my every day chores. I faced the challenge of learning to swallow my pride, and be honest and spell out my basic needs. I required assistance with dressing, showering, cutting up my food (and someone to catch it as it ran around my plate!)

Two things were clear to me, even at that early stage. I would need to walk the tenth mile before the majority of students would feel confident and comfortable about taking one step towards helping me. And I would have to learn not to impose myself solely upon one person, but recruit a team of helpers to assist me. I must allow God to open their eyes to meeting my needs, but in his timing, which did not necessarily coincide with my 'education' of them!

Finally, sleep did overtake me, but during the night my anxieties continued to haunt me in the most alarm-ing of nightmares. In my dream, it was next morning. I had arrived for my ten-minute input on how to relate to disabled people, all prepared and raring to go. But to my embarrassment, I'd steamed into the lecture room in my wheelchair, totally naked and frantically waving a bra above my head, yelling at the top of my voice, 'Somebody help—anybody!' No one had helped me dress. What a sight! What an uproar! And the callous words spoken the previous evening intruded into my nightmare: 'What demented person let her into the college?'

'Oh God,' I moaned, in my semi-conscious state. 'Please see to every little detail.' And then I slept.

It was 5.30 am and I was awake—wide awake! The sun filtered through the window, signalling the dawning of a new day. It was time to read, to pray and consciously yield myself to the Lord. Only then would I be able to face the day with confidence. I would steel myself to receive hurt and resentment. In return I was determined to show love as naturally and spontaneously as possible, and to exercise self-control—in short to turn the other cheek. College life wouldn't be easy, but prayer was the key. Without prayer I could do nothing. Prayer would give me God's peace and strength to cope—one day at a time.

On my knees, in the stillness of my little room, I prayed fervently. My confidence soared in the knowledge that God was with me, that here I was—miraculously at Bible college. I'd breeze through the day. God would take care of all the little details. . . .

My prayer time complete, my confidence buoyant, I busily prepared my ten-minute talk. I was determined I would help the students to understand disability. By sharing my experiences in America I would help them to develop sensitivity about healing—and non-healing.

As I sat at my desk, lost in thought, sketching out notes and an outline, I glimpsed a movement on my dressing gown which was hanging on the back of the door. Puzzled, I turned for a better view, and suddenly recoiled in horror as a mouse dropped onto the floor. My peaceful poise evaporated instantly as I let out a terrified shriek.

Almost immediately the door flew open and in rushed a startled looking student. I was too panic-stricken to talk—all I could do was point at the offending rodent. The tiny mouse was as scared as I was, frozen in the middle of the floor. Finally it scuttled out of the half-open door, straight over the toes of my fellow student.

Anne—I discovered her name later—took off, catapulting from the floor to my desk, then from the desk to my chair, screaming at the top of her voice, before flopping in a hysterical heap on my bed. Then, aware of her undignified behaviour, she buried her head in my pillow, stifling her giggles.

So much for my prayerful peace, self control and for Christian maturity! Waking up the whole dormitory was not an auspicious start, and no doubt I'd made more than a few enemies. I wondered if I would ever do anything right. Perhaps a shower would help me to regain my composure. So, still in my night-clothes, I propelled myself down the corridor, shoved through the heavy doors and into the showers. But the door proved too heavy for me, and as it shut on the back of my wheelchair it threw me out onto the cold concrete floor.

The physical pain as I grazed my knees was nothing compared with the inner struggle I felt as I looked at the shower cubicle. The step was at least a foot high— I'd break my neck climbing over it—and the controls were six feet up the wall, totally out of my reach. At home I could climb in and out of the bath and shower with little effort. At college it would be well-nigh impossible!

I looked around, panic-stricken once more. The shower block was empty and as quiet as a morgue. There was nobody to help me. I was stranded.

Managing to regain my chair, I quickly gathered up my toiletries and made a bee-line down the hallway. I knew one particular student was a nurse, so I stopped at her door and thumped hard on it. My nightmare was becoming hauntingly real. I was still undressed and unwashed. Would I really turn up in class with no clothes on? I flushed hot and cold, panic gripping me like a vice.

'Can't manage buttons, zips, bras,' I stammered as she opened her door. 'I need help dressing. Would you mind—*please?*' I was desperate. But the warmth and understanding for which I yearned was missing. She condescended to help me, but made it quite clear that it would be just this once as she was at Bible college to find 'her man'. Pausing, she moistened her lips, 'If I'm continually attending to you and your needs, my chances of finding the right husband will be severely hampered.'

I nearly fell out of my chair for the second time that morning. I was aware that Faith Bible College had been irreverently nick-named 'Faith Bridal College' by some, but I couldn't believe that people would go there just to find a spouse. But then weren't my own motives also questionable? My ultimate goal was to become more 'spiritual' so that I could return to America and be healed!

At that particular point in time, I wasn't concerned about anyone's motives for helping me. 'I just want to get dressed!' I was almost screaming.

I had a choice. Was I going to be a 'custard Christian' —one who gets upset over trifles, or was I going to accept her back-to-front offer of help for that day, and trust God for tomorrow? I chose to leave God with tomorrow and be thankful for today's help!

Miracles do happen. At 8.30 am, the time for devotions, I arrived in the lecture room, washed, fed and fully clothed. Relief flooded over me.

A wonderful time of praise and worship, a thirty-minute 'word' of encouragement from another student, and then I was wheeled centre-stage.

Despite my nervousness, the peace of God, which I had felt so strongly earlier that morning, was returning. Looking over the sea of faces I deliberately enunciated my words, regaining my confidence and composure as I did so—especially as the students seemed to show understanding as I spoke from personal experience. That morning I felt able to lay foundations upon which my relationships with the other students would be built over the next four-and-a-half months.

At least, that was my aim! Perhaps I'd been too hard-hitting, or maybe too realistic. Whatever the case, I sparked a barrage of ridiculous questions.

'Can you see the blackboard clearly?' one student asked, despite the fact that I sat in the front row, just feet away from it.

'Can you follow what is being said?' asked another, yelling as if I were deaf.

I had clearly explained that my handicaps were purely physical, and that hearing and sight were not among them. My speech was impaired, but I understood and could follow the lecturers without any difficulty—the same as any 'normal' person!

Eventually the penny dropped and the students' relief showed. I wasn't crazy after all! I became very aware of my need for patience as I explained yet again (and no doubt again in the days that followed) how to relate to a disabled person in basic terms.

As the morning's programme proceeded, barriers melted and the majority of my classmates finally began to reach out and relate to me as a person rather than as a disability.

The lectures were intensive—packed full of learning and thinking. The Lord's presence filled the classroom. I was electrified with excitement. 'What next, Lord?' I wondered. For four hours my spirit drank deeply, often absorbing more than my mind or emotions. The lecturers illustrated their teaching with examples from their own lives. They were absolutely honest, admitting their own inadequacies and exposing themselves to our judgement.

Sometimes the only sound in the class was the rustling of Bibles. On other occasions questions and answers shot back and forth, punctuated with laughter or applause at a particularly wise crack. I was immersed in a sea of activity and information, and loving every minute of it.

Even my note-taking problems were overcome. A fellow student agreed to do carbon copies of her notes. I thanked God for her. Without her skill and expertise, I doubt if I could have produced the standard of work expected. The college staff were also sensitive to my needs, often producing copies of their own notes to assist me with assignments. But apart from this they showed me no favouritism and gave me no concessions —not that I wanted any.

The eighteen-week Standard Training Course is a comprehensive course in Christian doctrines and principles. A number of selected books and bibliographies are studied, emphasising the practical application of the word of God to our daily lives. However, the course was sufficiently flexible to include a variety of subjects which provided a well-balanced instruction in christian discipleship and ministry training.

That first week at college was very intensive. We were expected to submit three written assignments which was an enormous task for me anyway. My load was compounded because that first Friday I was scheduled to lead the thirty-minute devotional period which sparked off each morning's lectures. I was determined to succeed at this, and pecked away at the keyboard of my electric typewriter until the early hours each morning. I got little sleep that first week! But all the preparation and hard work did eventually pay off.

On Friday, at 2.30 am, I rose from my bed to begin preaching my message—at the door-knob! I pronounced and perfected every word. My subject was 'Determination in God' and I spoke from the heart. Hours later it made its mark upon several fellow students, and I felt humbled yet very satisfied that I had achieved my week's goal—but, my, was I exhausted!

Although the course was very concentrated—there was always study, duties and assignments (naturally, I was exempt from duties), meetings to attend and sermons to prepare—there was also plenty of relaxation. There were furious games of table tennis and intense draughts matches; idle chatter in the kitchen, or simply leaning against a wall watching others.

The healing of personality clashes and tension between room-mates, the love that united different nationalities, men and women, married and single, young and older, the obedience to the demands of a schedule and the inner discipline that governed our freedom, the peace that settled fears about the future —all sprang out of the depths of an ever more intimate relationship between the Lord and ourselves —which was what Faith Bible College was all about.

A most important part of the training at Faith was the outstation programme. This gave students the opportunity to get out and put the week's lectures into practice.

Students travelled many miles in teams of five to preach, testify and sing in churches, youth camps and many other meetings. Almost all denominations opened their doors to 'Faith teams' and the college received good reports of the blessing the students had been. But most important was the extra experience in ministry that the team members received through this involvement.

I longed that I too could become a part of this ministry, but I needed to think practically. At the end of each day I was exhausted. By the end of a week I was bombed-out! Home was the best place for me. I needed to recover from the onslaught of the week. When I arrived home that first Friday night, I slept like a dead woman—sixteen hours in all!

My parents were marvellous. They attended to my practical needs—washing, spring-cleaning my room and transporting me to and from college. Mother also helped to provide illustrations for my written assignments whenever possible, as well as giving assistance with projects I may have struggled to finish in time.

College life taught me one lesson very early: I'd taken my parents for granted. No one understood quite like Mum and Dad.

Mother encouraged and cajoled me into sticking with it, even in the tough times, for it's in the tough times that our faith is strengthened. Each weekend, with Mother and Dad's support and encouragement, I would be sufficiently revived to face another week at college.

Kaye Hurn, Dean of women, busily organised a team of students to assist me with the practical details of each day. For this, and her commitment in assisting me to cope with the demands of a very heavy schedule I will always be eternally grateful. Within a few weeks, I never needed to ask for help, willing hands were always ready to push my chair and assist me in any way I needed. God answered prayer and over the weeks I found that 'his grace was sufficient for me' as I was able to adapt to the methods of each helper.

How did fifty-two strangers actually become my brothers and sisters, closer even than my natural family? It was by catching fire from one another as we gathered to pray for different parts of the world. Prayer was an essential and vital part of life at Faith Bible College. Students were encouraged to develop a consistent prayer life, and ample opportunities were given for them to discover this discipline. However, there were also plenty of occasions for corporate prayer. Every Friday morning students would get up early to pray together, seeking God and interceding for one another and for the nation. One evening per fortnight students divided into cell groups to pray for Faith graduates and the Lord's work in other parts of the world.

I loved these prayer times, believing that even from

a wheelchair one could be a great missionary. I could change an entire continent by fervent prayer! Some of my most memorable moments would be while praying, ranging around the world and upholding Christian work in far off countries.

At Faith everyone was invited to enter into a deeper experience of prayer. At least, that's what I thought—until the first cutting remark from my prayer cell leader. A highly intelligent, well-educated and well-presented lady, my presence totally threw her. She had a mental block about me which resulted in her treating me as a 'non-person'. For example, when taking the register, twenty-four present equalled twenty-five minus Margie!

I had expected to be encouraged to pray and her attitude exasperated me. I worked extemely hard at not allowing it to become too big to handle. But it was a battle to maintain a sweet spirit towards this lady, and stay close to God and not become discouraged or bitter. Through it all I learned never to underestimate the power of prayer. Despite the fact that it hurt me to be absent as far as she was concerned, I continued to come along and give verbal contribution to the group. Although it took time, (three months in all!) she gradually overcame her prejudices and began to respond sensibly towards me.

There were funny times as well as exasperating ones at Faith Bible College. I'll never forget one particular Monday evening. I'd returned to college after spending the weekend at home. Unknown to me, a problem had arisen with the plumbing in one of the toilets and it had been placed out of bounds. I hastily propelled myself to the toilets wanting to relieve my bladder before the evening's lectures began. The door slammed behind me and I scambled out of my chair and up onto the throne. Business finished, I reached up to flush the toilet. To my astonishment, instead of water going down, it gushed up. Surprised, saturated and too scared to move I began to yell my head off, trying to attract someone's attention.

Moments ticked by before the door was flung open. There stood one of my fellow students, a look of absolute dismay on her face. She looked at me. Then at the watery mess creeping towards her feet. Then she looked back at me again. Quietly and with a very straight face she asked, 'Well tell me, have you quite finished?'

We both dissolved into hysterical laughter as she padded through the overflow to rescue me.

From loo to lecture, I needed to learn to leave behind such moments of hilarity and adjust to the sobriety of the lecture room.

In the classroom, being in the front row, I often felt like a sitting duck. This was especially so when lecturers came to speak on healing—and reasons for non-healing.

One particular morning we had an overseas speaker. I listened with rapt attention as he talked on the subject of healing. He also had attended several Kathryn Kuhlman miracle services, and shared with us about her dynamic ministry and the supernatural encounters he had experienced in his own life.

Then, almost inevitably it seemed, he turned on me. 'Young lady,' he commanded, pointing his long finger directly at me, 'stand up!'

Behind me I heard the soft murmurs of my classmates, 'Yes, Jesus...Thank you, Jesus...Praise you, Lord...'

Stand up. I could have dropped dead! I wished the floor would open up and swallow me. In front of fifty students, totally unprepared, this man was demanding from me what hadn't been possible in my 10,000-miles-for-a-miracle pilgrimage. Long moments passed as the prayers continued fervently. Eventually, however, expectancy drifted away into embarrassed silence.

As the lecturer shifted from foot to foot, the hairs on

the back of my neck prickled as I felt 100 eyes burning into my back. I looked down and realised that this was the first day at Faith that I'd chosen to wear my yellow dress—the dress from the vision in which I would walk, run, skip and dance.

Finally morning tea break came, and as the students filed out, the lecturer quietly seated himself beside my chair.

'So, you've also been to Kathryn Kuhlman's services,' I rattled out as fast as I could. 'Remarkable lady, remarkable ministry... An experience I'll never forget ... Returned from the States just recently myself.'

His face collapsed and his eyes brimmed with tears. 'I'm sorry,' he whispered, his voice choked. 'I didn't know. It must have been devastating...terribly disappointing for you.'

I nodded, unable to speak.

Without further words, he stood, slid the chair back under the desk and left the room, wiping his eyes and blowing his nose. He'd be a wiser man in the future.

The yellow dress had to go! The very next day I donated it to a sale, the proceeds going to the Crippled Children's Society.

It had only been on the table for a few minutes when an attractive young woman picked it up and asked if she could try it on. A few minutes later she bought it. My heart was full as I watched her skip then dance out of the building in my dress—the dress in which I was never able to skip and dance. She looked so like myself, or at least so like what I would have looked like if I could have skipped and danced.

As she left with my dress, something inside me died. The vision was dead. Late that afternoon, when we returned to college, the rest of the vision disintegrated. We received the news that Kathryn Kuhlman had died.

With her death came the death of my dreams. My yellow dress had gone. Kathryn Kuhlman had gone.

I would never return to America to be healed.

10

The Heavenly Visitor

I dropped from my chair to the floor, and kneeling by my bed, I cried uncontrollably. The room was silent. Kathryn Kuhlman was dead. My yellow dress was sold. My vision had gone.

'God,' I agonised, 'I'm so confused! I don't want to leave this place the same as I entered it, no good to you or man. I'll do anything, Lord, go anywhere, but please, dear God, don't throw me on the scrap heap.'

My Bible lay open on the bed, and as I glanced at it, the words of a verse leapt out at me: 'I tell you the truth,' I read through misty eyes, 'unless an ear of wheat falls to the ground and dies, it remains only a single seed. But if it dies, it produces many seeds' (Jn 12:24). I needed to die—to my own desires, self-interest and self-concern. Yet I was afaid to do so. Alone in my room, I remonstrated with God. 'Oh God, must I die to self? Why are you silent? What do you think you're doing?' Sobs wracked my body, utterly exhausting me.

Today I never cease to be amazed at God's tolerance. Yet as I lay there, raging in that room, he saw me and understood everything—the pain, the hurt, the anger. Finally, in the early hours of the morning, the break-through came as I let go, releasing my pent-up feelings. I heaved myself to my knees and looked out of the small bedroom window at the dark sky. It was the moment of truth. I could no longer remain in some kind of fool's paradise. The reality was that I would *never* walk, nor *dance*, in my lovely yellow dress.

'O God,' I cried out, 'allow your Spirit to touch my life. Don't let me dodge the difficulties. Help me face death to self. If, deep within me, you see that I am a corn of wheat afraid to die, help me face the fact.'

As I prayed, something swept the room. The curtains rustled, as if moved by some mysterious breath. The Spirit of God then swept through me, baptising me with love.

Like a dam bursting, words of joy tumbled out of my mouth. I felt totally released and free, almost intoxicated as God's overwhelming love filled my being. There was no need to struggle or concentrate on my wayward speech. I thanked him and praised him—and loved him! And as the love for God welled up in my heart, so did a special love for those around me. I had had personality clashes and misunder-standings with other students, but that night in my room I repented of my critical attitude, and my demands on them when they too were struggling to find their way through college. I now loved them for who they were, not for what they did for me.

As love for God and love for my fellow students developed, I also came to love myself. Now I realised why I was so bitter and frustrated—I was embarrassed about myself and my disability. I did not love myself—not as God intended. So how could I expect students to accept me if I didn't accept myself the way God made me?

Finally, exhausted, I choked out, 'I believe you Jesus...thank you for not healing me in America!' Then I laughed—there's healing in laughter. And I cried—there's healing in tears too. I was at last reaching the stage where God could use me. Later I realised that this experience had taken place exactly a year to the day after my experience of forced praise at the Kathryn Kuhlman meeting. Today, praise was in no way forced, but natural, spontaneous and freeing, coming from the depths of my being.

When I arrived at class the next morning, I was red-eyed from hours of weeping and lack of sleep. As the lecture began, something swept the room. A white mist descended as the awesome breath of the Holy Spirit filled the building. Softly, ever so softly, voices joined in singing, 'Something good is going to happen today, happen today, this very hour...Jesus of Nazareth is passing your way.'

I couldn't sing; I couldn't do anything except sob. Through my muffled cries and the mist I could dimly hear the tutor saying, 'He's here, here in this room, for you. You don't need me. Reach out and touch him.'

That morning Jesus of Nazareth walked through the aisles and between the desks, touching students along the way. To one he gave a vision of the cross, to another a vision of his glory. It was holy ground. There was silence. One hardly dared breathe. All heads were bowed. Some dropped to the floor. Some wept. Some just sat or stood stunned. I sobbed.

In front of me was a dark blackboard covering the whole length of the wall. Suddenly I sensed that something was near me so I looked up. My eyes fell on a majestic white horse. On the horse sat a rider dressed in a flowing purple cloak with elaborate gold braiding. His hair was jet black, tangled and matted with blood. His cheeks were black and blue where fingernails had clawed their way through his flesh.

My heart was in my mouth, thumping so loudly that I felt everybody in the room must have heard it. I gazed, transfixed by his disfigurement. I needed no explanation. In an instant I knew the rider was Jesus and his disfigurement was the result of my lashing out, my clawings, my frustrations, my anger, my bitterness over not being healed.

His eyes drew me like a magnet. They were so soft,

so tender, so full of love and free from condemnation. I felt as if his gaze entered the very depths of my being, transmitting love and compassion, soothing and healing the turmoil in the very depths of my soul.

The rider reached down and touched my shoulder, sending a surge of power through my body. I was unable to remain upright, and slumped across my desk. Time ticked by. How much time I don't know. The sense of power subsided and I looked down and found the rider kneeling before me pulling an ugly, heavy black garment down my body and off my feet— the garment of bitterness. As he stood up he seemed to draw me up with him and I felt wrapped in an amazing invisible robe, like a shaft of laser light, that brought cleansing throughout my being.

I looked up again. The rider had changed as well. He now wore white robes himself. His hair was golden and flowing. His face was unblemished.

His eyes penetrated mine with the message: 'I understand. It has been a big disappointment. But it is time to be the woman I've created you to be. It is more important to me to see spiritual growth and maturity than to see a comfortable, co-ordinated body. Whether I have lived up to your expectations or not, like everyone else you too will bow the knee and confess that I am King of kings and Lord of lords.' Then he vanished.

It was hours before the campus returned to its normal noisy self. Many other students had experienced dynamic encounters similar to my own. We hardly dared speak of them, they were so precious. I wept for all those months filled with bitterness and wrong attitudes. And I prayed for a deeper understanding of God's will for my life. I believed that all that had happened in America was an important part of his plan.

I bowed my head, my heart and my whole being, humbling myself before him and worshipping him. I mulled over the mystery of this great God. I had been unwilling to bend to the purposes of God, and the person who is unwilling to bend must be broken. God is sovereign. He cannot be limited. Yet I had measured him by my intellect. I knew God could heal supernaturally, but now I realised that it was sometimes part of his plan not to heal supernaturally.

As I sat deep in thought, trying to piece my life together and understand God's overall plan, I was interrupted. My good friend Darryl called into my room.

'Hi,' he greeted, his misty blue eyes communicating warmth and openness. 'God did something special today, didn't he?'

As I related my vision to him, we both sensed that God was at work in my life. Although only twenty years old, Darryl had a maturity and perceptiveness well beyond his years. He also had a self-assurance which was most evident when he talked to me. Many students were uncomfortable with my chair, but Darryl was completely at ease and made me feel comfortable too.

He joked that he had a disability of his own—he was a PK (pastor's kid). His father's congregation had placed too high a standard on him and this had eventually resulted in rebellion. His mother had prayed for him and eventually Darryl turned back to God. His experiences had given him sensitivity and understanding. He knew how it felt to be an odd one out, and had a deep insight into other people's problems and needs. I liked Darryl.

He lowered himself onto a stool and leaned back against the wall, facing me.

'I felt the urge to talk to you,' he opened. 'You've experienced difficult times. Life breaks us all, but it's a fact of life that the place in which a bone breaks can heal so strongly that it will never break there again. We don't need to be ashamed of being broken.'

He hesitated, watching for my response. 'If that

happens in the natural, why not in the spiritual as well? Margie, the Bible tells us that it's from *weakness* that we are made strong. Hey, Marg, God's an expert at taking our weaknesses and turning them into strengths. He specialises in things we thought were impossible.'

Darryl's enthusiasm was infectious. I could see his point. Those areas where I was weakest could well become my strongest when I committed them to God for healing.

I was eager for more, and Darryl related stories of things that had taken place in his church back home.

'We've seen God's Spirit make a lot of people really come alive. One couple was on the verge of divorce. God did an amazing work in their lives and brought them back together again. One guy was high on dope and into all sorts of weird occult practices and Christ saved him. A girl I knew was all messed up inside, but God brought her inner healing. You should see her today.'

Darryl's stories came like rapid fire, each proving his point—God could heal the breaks in our lives and make them incredibly strong.

'Look,' he said, sipping his coffee, 'there are so many people who are so broken by life that they feel an overwhelming weakness. 'Marg, you can identify with those people. You could minister to the depths of their needs far better than I can. Better than anyone I know.

'Take heart,' he said, impishly pinching my cheek. 'God specialises in situations that are hopeless. There are no hopeless situations, only people who have grown hopeless about them. By his transforming power you'll become strong at the broken place!'

There was something about Darryl that I admired; and I wanted it in my own life. He radiated confidence and authority. He spoke convincingly of the Lord's purposes—purposes he believed God had for his life and mine.

Over the weeks and months at college, Darryl and I

grew very close. He was a stimulating conversationalist, and he helped me broaden my thinking by discussing a wide range of subjects—from sport to politics to avenues of ministry. He also helped me in many practical ways.

The experience in my room following the death of Kathryn Kuhlman, the vision of the white horse, and Darryl's constant encouragement and guidance led to a time of real growth for me at Faith. Classmates and staff members increasingly encouraged me, praying with me and for me to achieve my potential. I even had opportunities to put the theory into practice by speaking at public meetings.

My respect for those around me blossomed. And I marvelled at the sheer luxury of having so many months purely devoted to studying God's word, being surrounded by fellow Christians and living in such beautiful buildings, nestled between the hills and the sea. But I was still restless. My life seemed hollow and narrow in outlook, and I felt a deep and unfulfilled yearning.

A constant stumbling-block to my Christian growth was a tendency to over-react when the subject of healing was taught or discussed. Some days remarks floated over my head. At other times they felt like daggers plunged into my heart.

When this happened, I used Darryl as a sounding board. We talked through the hurt and frustration. He helped because he understood. He would be honest and firm with me, but he'd think carefully before responding.

'Listen,' he would say, leaning forward from behind my chair and brushing his cheek against mine in affection, 'it is ignorance, lack of understanding. People just need educating. Over-reacting won't help.' His voice had a soothing effect. 'You know you're loved—wheelchair, disability, hysterical outbursts, the lot! It's no big deal to me. You're Margie and I love you. You must learn to accept yourself, to overcome and not be got at. If you don't, you'll never make it in ministry.'

Some weeks later, this time during morning devotions, my gaze towards the blackboard was again interrupted by another very clear vision. I saw myself in a beautiful flowing dress on a platform. I was Kathryn Kuhlman the second—healed, perfectly co-ordinated, with perfect speech. My preaching was powerful. I walked and skipped about the stage, preaching authoritatively to a huge crowd. But some-how I sensed that something was wrong. 'Lord, show me what's wrong,' I cried.

'Stop and look,' was his commanding reply. It was then that I really saw my congregation. They were somehow vacant. Many of them were disabled physically, some crippled, some in wheelchairs, some with crutches or canes. Others were emotionally disabled as a result of hurts, loss, stress, divorce and abuse.

The second part of the vision I had that day was like a video of the banquet Jesus described in Luke 14. I saw an enormous table beautifully laid out but devoid of guests. A voice boomed out from the sky, 'Go into the highways and byways and bid the blind, lame, maimed and halt to come and dine.' My mind recalled, in an instant, the call I'd sensed on my life during the time I struggled to live when feeling the imminency of death. 'I have appointed you and chosen you to this specific task and if you don't do it, it will remain undone.'

I knew that day what the 'task' was. My responsibility was to evangelise the disabled and help the church to accommodate them, accept them, relate to them and minister to them. Somehow we needed to establish an organisation to meet the needs of the disabled and to develop their potential. I was confronted by the fact that my aim had been limelight and self-glory, not reaching to the depths of people's needs.

The significance of this vision became more apparent as time went on. I was still hankering to be free from my wheelchair, failing to see how it fitted in with my concept of ministry.

God was speaking to me, not in whispers, but in thunderous tones. I wanted to see him in the spectacular, not the commonplace. But it is in the everyday things of life that people find Jesus—in prisons, refugee camps, with the sick and the outcasts. I had approached my spiritual life with a preconceived idea of what I wanted to do for God, yet he was telling me in unmistakable terms that he was not through with my life, that he wanted to use me. The only problem was that his plans for my life were very different from mine.

'Lord, why do you always have to have your way?' I grumbled. 'What about my way for a change?'

Then I considered the life of Jesus—how in the Garden of Gethsemane he had groaned in anguish, 'Father, if you are willing, take this cup from me; yet not my will, but yours be done' (Lk 22:42). And on the cross cried out, 'My God, my God, why have you forsaken me?' (Mt 27:46).

What a release that gave! If Jesus Christ could hurl such questions at his heavenly Father, how much more can we? The voice of God was crystal clear—lay aside the physical miracle and accept a ministry.

I began to experience something of what Peter must have felt when the Lord questioned him as he held out those fish.

'Do you truly love me more than these?' Jesus asked then (Jn 21:15).

'Margie, do you love me more than walking and dancing in a yellow dress?' he was asking me now. 'Do you love me more than having a career, more than a marriage?'

I wrestled with mixed emotions, weighing up my answers. I couldn't bring myself to believe that God wasn't going to heal me, but that he was charging me with the responsibility of establishing a ministry that would meet the needs of the disabled.

But hadn't I promised to do anything and to go anywhere for God?

After the lecture was over that morning I went back to the prayer room and continued to struggle. Several other students were also there, and we joined to pray for a young man who was being challenged to go on an outreach to an unpleasant environment. God gave one of the staff members a vision.

It was a flower, and each petal of the flower was facing inwards so that its real beauty wasn't visible to the world. This flower shook me to the core. I knew it represented me. I was for ever looking inwards, trying to have changes made in my body while people outside were suffering and without hope.

The petals of my life were facing in and not out as they should have been. Tears streamed down my face. What about my relationship with Jesus Christ and my attitude towards the Great Commission?

Lord, I love you,' I stammered. 'You know I love you. I will do it!'

I felt a pair of hands lightly touch my head as one of the staff began to pray for me.

'The church needs your voice,' he prophesied. 'There are hundreds of people who still live in institutions. They are in wheelchairs. They live in the clutches of fear and depression. They are angry, rejected by society. They need a strong prophetic voice that will point them to Christ—someone who will give them their only way out of frustration, misery and helplessness.'

'They will not hear eloquent preachers. The majority will never attend a large church, and would not be welcome if they did. The disabled need a prophetic voice from their own ranks. You understand their speech. You live where they live. You can identify with them. God has touched your life. He has called you and chosen you so you can win others and call others to follow the way of the cross. And he wants you to be a voice to the church for the disabled. Margie, this day we as a body of people declare you to be that prophetess.'

There was only one reply I could give: 'Lord, I surrender.'

11

Running with a Vision

Graduation was over. Everyone was a little sad, but it was also time to thank God for our teachers and all the experiences we had been through—help, growth, deliverance and inner healing.

Stepping into new adventures could be traumatic. For me Faith Bible College was the launching pad for a ministry born through visions, teaching and prophetic commission.

I was twenty-eight years old, and I had a strong conviction that what I had learned in the classroom would now be tested in the real world. I couldn't continue to live in a 'spiritual incubator' for the rest of my life. My wholehearted desire was to obey the Lord: to step out into new ventures to help others, disabled people, with dreams and visions of their own.

I was daunted by the prospect of beginning a ministry among the disabled. Even though I'd lived with disability all my life, I was quite unaware of the many nitty-gritty issues disabled people face every day.

I remember attending a film evening on the life and work of Mother Teresa in the slums of Calcutta. I felt overwhelmed as I watched the seething mass of humanity, the poverty, starvation and suffering. Everywhere hands stretched out in desperate need. How in the world could one person begin to reach the

137

depth of human need or the depth of human suffering that the masses presented?

Suddenly a man who was watching beside me jumped to his feet and yelled, 'Christ is the answer! There's hope!' His words, so glib and unrealistic, stabbed me, reminding me how easily we spiritualise and even neglect the practical 'good works' Jesus predestines for us as his disciples.

As I pondered the work of Mother Teresa I reflected on the plight of many disabled people. Christ was the answer, yes. But not just in the spiritual dimension. Christ also had to be the answer in the practical aspects of everyday life. Life for them was fraught with countless frustrations: loneliness, hope-lessness, despair, depression, sexual frustration, lack of creative outlets, isolation. We needed to communicate Christ as the answer to all these questions and issues.

I was a disabled person who had experienced the overwhelming love and grace of God. But I'd also known the luxury of the support of a wonderful family and friends who cared for me faithfully, whether by lifting my spirits or lifting me into my chair. Beyond my cosy environment were hundreds, perhaps thousands, of disabled people who had experienced none of this. Some, because they were too great a burden for their families, were shifted from one institution to another. They not only required spiritual help but practical caring—and from God's people. I knew I'd been 'chosen' to give it, but just how did I translate such a dream into everyday reality?

I'd struggled with anger when well-meaning Christians invited the disabled along to church services as a target for physical healing. Their intentions may have been good, but there was no understanding for the disabled as real feeling people, nor any realisation of the guilt and sense of failure that were experienced when no healing took place. It was a matter of be healed and 'hallelujah' or be swept out of sight with other unanswered prayers!

From personal experience I found that more conservative congregations, while not emphasising healing, would invite the disabled to a magnificent Christmas banquet then, having done their annual good deed, forget about them for the rest of the year.

However, it wasn't my intention to bring condemnation on the church, but to raise questions by bringing the words of Jesus to them: 'Are you living *my* life among the disabled?'

As incredible as it seemed, my ministry began in Auckland. My friend Di was excited and more than enthusiastic to launch out into a new venture with me. We grew closer together as we strove to meet the undeniable need for a Christian organisation in New Zealand which would cater for and meet the needs of all types of disability.

Over numerous cups of tea, Di and I discussed ways we could penetrate the highways and byways. The task before us was enormous. We couldn't possibly go it alone—we needed help. Having a vision can be exciting, but we needed many people to flesh it out if we were going to reach the depth of human need.

We had no doubts that we'd find dozens of disabled folk in institutions, hospitals and their own private homes all over the city who'd be all too willing to enjoy an outing, a dinner party and meet together for fun, fellowship and a time of mutual sharing. But finding able-bodied people who would give up time in their busy schedules to provide transport for our disabled friends posed another challenge.

As I bounced ideas around, Di picked up those ideas, moulded them and put them into action. We sensed we were forging into virgin territory, touching on something that would express God's love in a unique and powerful way. We discussed a fellowship which would cater for the *whole person*—spiritually, mentally, physically, socially.

I aimed high. I dreamed of a fellowship no longer divided by the gifted and the ungifted, the likely and the unlikely, the abled and the disabled. I dreamed of a fellowship comprised of people caring compassionately for others because of Jesus and his response to the poor, needy and afflicted. I often meditated on the Book of Proverbs which is full of warnings to those who neglect to provide and care for the needs of the poor and afflicted.

It was not to be a sympathy ministry, but an empathy and answer ministry, where the disabled could be drawn to Christ; one in which they could share, not just with other handicapped people, but with the able-bodied and the community; one in which they could speak, write, communicate their faith, talents, hurts, dreams and passions.

'Marg, you're dreaming of a perfect church!' cautioned a friend.

'Well, Jesus is going to return one day...for his perfect church!' I responded positively, only to hear a voice retort: 'Well, he sure won't be returning in a hurry!'

Chuckles followed. Imparting a vision isn't easy. My heart knotted. I wanted so much to say the right things, to do the right things. I wanted not just to dream, but to practise ways of helping my disabled friends. I wanted the best for them. But I had so much to learn.

Neither Di nor I knew what lay ahead, but together we shared a dream and we were totally dependent upon God to bring that dream to reality. Barriers confronted us on all sides. Barriers of fear, inadequacy, embarrassment and ignorance—all needed to be broken down. Many people keep the disabled at a distance. After all, how do you converse with someone who cannot speak? How do you lift a person out of a car and into a wheelchair, or empty a legbag?

We needed people who would go to the same lengths as the four friends went to for their paralytic friend in Mark's Gospel; people whose yearning to meet human need made them push through crowds, scale walls and tear off roofs. Although healing is wonderful, it is not necessarily a priority for the disabled. I believe that the motive of the paralytic man's friends was 'quality of life'. Disabled people can have, and give, quality of life from their wheelchairs.

Though I was still living with my parents in the Bay of Plenty, I made many trips to Auckland. From the Willis' home, Di and I spent hours on the telephone to institutions, hospitals and rest homes, making personal contact with disabled folk. Di, being an occupational therapist, also had contact with other therapists and her former patients, whereas I knew several disabled people from days spent living in or visiting institutions. Among them were old friendships and acquaintances I longed to renew. From this base we began our penetration into the highways and byways, compelling them to 'come, dine at a mini-banquet'!

The meal was a combined effort. Di enlisted the help of friends to prepare a 'special dish' (institutions do not serve fancy foods!) and also be available for transport and assistance in bringing folk to the meal being held in the Willis' huge lounge.

With the 'kick-off' in sight excitement escalated. However, getting involved in the 'real world' of the disabled can prove daunting, as I found out when visiting the Laura Ferguson Trust Home to invite my friend Larry Cox to our evening.

Larry and I had met in an institution years before. My stay was for a brief assessment, whereas Larry's was long term. Larry's mother had died in childbirth. His father had died a year later and Larry had been brought up by an elderly grandmother who by now had also died. He had no family. He'd never known the freedom of life outside hospital care, and over the years he'd suffered terrible cruelty. I looked forward to sharing my faith with Larry. He'd always found a soft spot in my heart. I longed to share my inner healing and the faith I'd experienced amid despair.

But I found Larry was in no mood for platitudes.

'God,' he hissed at me, the first time I broached the subject. 'Who's God? Certainly not a personal being who cares about individuals. Bible verses are too glib to have anything but surface meaning. Try and apply "For God worketh all things for good" to the days when we were in that special assessment ward! I'd like to know where God was when all that awful stuff happened to us.'

My mind flashed back fifteen years. I remembered only too well what Larry was referring to. The trained staff, all of the highest calibre and dedication, worked for our highest good. However, once they marched off duty, the ward often became a nightmare. Most nurse aides were tolerant, sensitive and caring, but some were downright sadistic.

Like Miss Sarah. She flayed us with her tongue, making obscene comments about our bodies and brains. Sometimes she'd completely lose control, lifting a disabled child high into the air, tormenting him and then dropping him onto the floor. She particularly picked on the younger disabled—defenceless children who were prone to fits and seizures—delighting in watching them hit the floor, then gag and froth in uncontrollable frenzy.

'Bastards!' Larry shrieked, years of pent-up hatred bursting out as he relived indignities he and others had suffered.

Miss Sarah would remove short straps from his calipers and, for no reason at all, whip him with the buckle ends. Larry's legs and buttocks often sported great welts and bruising, but he never dared to complain or report her.

She continually threatened him. 'If you ever say anything against me, you —— , I'll see that you pay for it dearly! Do you understand?' It was no idle threat. Larry was terrified that something even more horrible would happen to him if he complained.

It had taken months, even years, for me to forgive my enemies, including Miss Sarah, and learn to love them. Even then I could only forgive because of God's supernatural love. Larry had suffered much more than I and, in himself, forgiveness was impossible.

As I struggled for an adequate reply to his tirade, we were joined by Max Clarke, a bright young quadriplegic who'd been listening in to our conversation. His muscles wouldn't quite support his head, so it dropped slightly to the right. But his voice, mind and spirit were strong. He mounted a new attack on my over-simplified Christian witness.

'I've done a lot of reading and studying,' he announced. 'I've looked at religion, philosophy, everything. God is just a "crutch" some people use. That's their only way of coping. For me, life has absolutely no meaning. It's pointless. Absurd.'

'Then why bother?' I countered, still shaken by Larry's vehemence. 'Why not commit suicide? In fact, why doesn't the whole human race commit suicide if life has no meaning?'

'Oh, I suppose it can have meaning. As I explained, some people use God as a crutch—that gives meaning to life. But let's be realistic—when the chips are down, like for us here, you see how shallow religion is.'

'But do you think life makes sense?'

'Probably not for us. People on their feet can eat, work, make love—all kinds of things. Pursuit of happiness. Y'know.'

I nodded.

'But here, well, that's a different story. We've

reduced life to its barest elements. And for the most part, there's no real reason to live.'

'Then why are you still alive?'

'Max shrugged. 'Guess I'm not gutsy enough to do myself in. Besides, I guess life can have meaning if you find it for yourself.'

'How?'

'Your mind. Intelligence. I get a kick out of developing my mind. To hell with my body. Maybe I can find something in being intelligent.'

'Maybe,' I offered. 'But what about everyone else? Everyone on their feet? They're born. They live and die with existence as their only goal. Why bother?'

'You've got me, Margie,' he answered. 'Why not read some of my books by Sartre, Marx and other great minds?'

'I have,' I answered honestly. 'They all pointed me further and further from God and hope. The meaning of life was that it had no meaning. Life without an eternal focus, without God, leads to despair.'

Max was cheerful enough, even positive, but his tragic accident and institutional life had robbed him of any openness to a God who was supposed to care.

'God,' Larry cut across again. 'I'll never see God in a person. Some people have minds worse than animals. If I ever see God, maybe he's in a rose, a sunset, or the sea—but never in a person!'

Max, spurred on by Larry's vehemence, scornfully declared: 'I'll never make love again. Why should I believe in God? And what's he going to do if I don't believe—damn me to hell? I'm already in hell! No, there's no God, Margie. I'll never be on my feet again. There's nothing to live for that has any real meaning. God's dead!'

By the time these two guys had finished, I felt shot apart. My well-meaning 'come to Jesus' prattle lay in tatters! I was embarrassed—my answers sounded so glib, so empty. They saw straight through me. How could my dreams of helping others with disabilities become a reality unless I knew how to communicate God's love and put it into practice with people like Larry and Max?

Again my heart knotted. I felt their frustration and pain, but what hurt most was realising I had no acceptable answers. Disdainfully they rejected my invitation.

By the time Di arrived on the scene, disappointment was written all over my face. In silence she pushed my chair through the glass doors and down the long corridor to the carpark. I absorbed myself in the rhythmic squeak of my rubber wheels on the shiny linoleum.

To expect people to pattern their lives after my own was unrealistic. Things didn't happen for others the way they had for me. Yet in some unique way they needed to meet God for themselves. I wanted to cry, not for myself, but for guys like Larry and Max. I wanted so much to help, but was powerless to do so.

'They've got a lot to learn,' I voiced out loud.

'Haven't we all?' Di chipped in. She'd regularly worked with Max a few years back, and her comments added a healthy perspective. 'Don't take it too much to heart,' she encouraged. 'It'll take time. Never underestimate the power of prayer—it's got to be God! We'll win those guys somehow—just wait and pray.'

My visit to the Laura Ferguson Home was perhaps the turning point in establishing a ministry. It made me examine my heart, my motives and my message. I wanted to love, to help people as individuals. Each person was unique and faced their own set of challenges. Larry and Max were people, but I'd allowed them to become a project.

In the days that followed, I watched and listened as Di worked with the disabled—people who were shifted from one institution to the next; people who felt they were nothing but a burden in life. She took the time to communicate with a young spastic girl, or speak to a mother with a disabled child. I watched her kneel on the floor to adjust the strap of an elderly man's caliper. Everyone was treated as special. And people loved her in return.

As I watched Di, I reflected upon my own call to ministry. God's word had been personal and clear: 'I have chosen you. You are appointed to fulfil an important task. If you don't do it, it will remain undone...The disabled need a prophetic voice out of their own rank. You are that voice. You've lived where they live. God has called you so that you can win others. ...' But where did I actually begin? There was so much need, so few people committed to meeting that need.

In-depth discussions led to the planning of future programmes: a boat trip, picnics, gospel concerts, evangelical outreaches. But these weren't going to be enough. They were a start, but they would only bring interim relief. Many disabled people would still be forced to return to their unpleasant environments, where life was no picnic and one cruel comment or action could instantly destroy any positive spiritual input we might have begun to cultivate.

We had to think practically, yet at the same time I sensed God challenging us to think big. I wanted to get rid of every institution in the country. 'Love Homes' were essential—caring, stimulating Christian family environments where the disabled could enjoy extended periods out of institutional life. Camps were needed for greater individual attention and the challenge of outdoor and recreational activities; and radio broadcasts were a must both for the disabled and to educate the able-bodied.

We envisaged a Christian foundation, offices and rooms for housing tape and book libraries, and special vans for transporting our disabled folk to and from activities. The scope of the need could have easily

defeated us before we began. In the natural, some
goals did seem impossible. Here we were, unskilled,
untrained, lacking business acumen and dreaming
lofty dreams with no known resources to draw from.
But our spirits were enlivened by it all. As Solomon
said, 'Without a vision the people perish.'

People need a vision. The person who is gripped by
a vision will be inspired to run and live with enthusiasm
and zeal. The prophet, Habakkuk, described such a
person: 'Then the Lord replied: "Write down the
revelation and make it plain on tablets so that a herald
may run with it"' (Hab 2:2). Vision is not wishful
thinking, vision is something concrete. Vision is having
your spiritual eyes open so that those things which are
not visible to most are more real to you than the
natural world around you. I believe that vision
translates God's word into reality.

Elijah the prophet knew God was going to bring rain
after a three-year drought. Though there where no
natural signs of rain he told King Ahab to go eat and
drink in preparation of that rain. He acted as if the
rain was already a reality and he ran to Jezreel (1 Kings
18:41–46). God's purpose in giving us vision is not that
we sit back and wait for it, but rather that we run with
the vision.

Abraham left the country in which he was born to go
to a country he had only seen with spiritual eyes—the
nation he was going to father, even when God required
that he sacrifice his own son.

In the same way, God challenged and encouraged us
to launch out, and carried us along on a sea of
inexplicable peace.

The night for our mini-banquet arrived. With able-
bodied drivers transporting the disabled, cars began
rolling up to the house. Every kind of paraphernalia
invaded the Willis' lounge that evening: disabled
people using walking sticks, white canes and wheelchairs, others scooting around in motorised chairs, and

yet others arriving with helmets, head-wands and communication boards. Noisy chatter buzzed around the room, accompanied by the mechanical sounds of chairs and the rubbing, knocking noise of artificial limbs and supports.

I observed Di and Hugh as they worked. Their hands communicated love and compassion as they gently lifted a young spastic man into his wheelchair, guided a blind man to his seat, or stretched the sore spastic muscles of an elderly lady, stiff from years of inactivity.

Surprisingly, at our first gathering, a multitude of unforeseen barriers confronted us. For example, the interaction between those with differing disabilities— the blind struggling to relate to those with cerebral palsy; cerebral palsy folk clashing with the intellectually handicapped (cerebral palsy sufferers are often thought to be mentally impaired and therefore resent being associated with the intellectually handicapped). Likewise, those with multiple sclerosis were struggling to cope with those who had muscular dystrophy.

However, just as God does not separate Jew and Greek, male and female, neither does he separate the blind and those with cerebral palsy, those with multiple sclerosis and those with muscular dystrophy. Our destiny is to become 'one in the bond of love'.

One-to-one support was vital. Care needed to be taken to match the maturity of the helper with the severity of the handicap. The helpers, most of whom were not professional therapists or nurses, quickly learned how to communicate, feed and otherwise care for their new friends.

During the course of the evening we also learned that several of our guests were extremely talented. Sure they lived with great physical problems, but what potential lay dormant below the surface! God could turn their problems into possibilities. Their disabilities could become doors into exciting ministries.

As I shared my dream with those gathered there, the atmosphere became electric. It provided a spark that ignited their spirits. I am convinced that if we could, we would have physically stood and declared our cause that night. Such was our unity of spirit. We sensed that we were on the threshold of something radical and revolutionary!

Amazingly, from this small yet talented group of diners, came the nucleus of a fellowship—pebbles that when cast into the pond of the disabled world sent out ripples spreading far and wide.

The twenty-five grew to fifty, the fifty to eighty-four, with a total of twenty wheelchairs—and we all crammed into the Willis' lounge, like sardines in a tin. We spilled into the kitchen and the hallway, some of us even balanced precariously on window sills. Helpers breathed silent prayers that no one in a wheelchair would want to use the bathroom. There was absolutely no room to manoeuvre.

As this meeting, people openly repented of fears, hang-ups and preconceived ideas about disabilities—and acknowledged embarrassment. This openness brought even more healing, bridging years of segregation and hurt.

Let's be honest. It's not appetising watching a cerebral palsied person trying to feed himself. Sometimes a bib and a mop are as vital as a knife and fork.

Neither is it easy to carry on a conversation with someone whose words are no more than a series of grunts and groans.

Compelling the disabled to 'come and dine' posed few problems. Arriving safely at the destination was a completely different matter, as one gallant helper discovered.

She'd volunteered to act as a chauffeur and was assigned to collect four disabled people, transporting them from one side of our sprawling city to the other. The starting point was in Central Auckland, and the first passenger, a severely cerebral palsied Maori girl, Shirley, lived in the southern part of the city—in the sticks!

Houses, factories and signposts disappeared and our bewildered helper began to wonder whether she'd been sent on a wild goose chase. Then a marae (a Maori community) appeared. After several enquiries at different dwellings, she finally found the invited guest.

However, Shirley was unable to talk or do anything for herself, and so our helper was subjected to a crash course in how to load a disabled person into a car and then fold and pack in their wheelchair (it's easy when you know how!).

Collecting the other three guests posed no major hurdles. But once all the passengers were securely belted in their seats, a new problem loomed on the horizon. For in the car was Shirley and another girl who couldn't speak, a girl who couldn't see, and yet another girl who spoke well, but had no idea of their destination. However, they did arrive, though rather late. But how the driver ever managed to reach her destination still remains a mystery.

The fellowship snowballed far quicker than we'd anticipated, and in order to cope we needed to get really organised. So we formed a committee for our group—the Christian Fellowship for Disabled (CFFD). Together we planned our next event, a gospel concert, and turned our sights from private homes to public venues.

Over 200 people rolled into the Foundation for the Blind recreational centre. One could sense the excitement as the lights dimmed and the band began playing 'God is so good, he's so good to me. . .' Everyone joined in, though not necessarily in tune! They sang it once, then twice, over and over. Then another chorus, and another, until the whole room pulsated with music.

The more co-ordinated people clapped and tapped

in time with the music, while others moved heads and limbs in delight—enjoying a release all too rare for so many imprisoned in disability. You could see their faces lighting up, vibrant with joy.

Suddenly, from out of the crowd, four strapping male helpers hoisted Patricia, in her wheelchair, high into the air and on to the stage. What in the world could someone as severely disabled as Patricia do at a concert?

Every eye focused on the shy teenager. She looked so vulnerable. In the background, a pianist started softly playing 'Something beautiful, something good'. An expectant hush descended as Patricia, with a clear, sweet voice, began singing. You could have heard a pin drop.

It was a poignant moment when she sang, 'All my confusion he understood.' A ripple of a cheer broke out as she sang the final line: 'Yet, he's made something beautiful out of my life!' More than a few eyes glistened as the crowd applauded loud and long. Once lifted from the stage Patricia seemed to sit just a little taller in her chair. She beamed with pleasure, knowing her talent was recognised and appreciated.

The concert proceeded with Mark, an accomplished guitarist, singing gospel ballads. Between songs, he spoke encouragingly of how people could overcome disability, heartache and emotional hurts. He shared the victory we have in Jesus from his own experience of disability—blindness. Being disabled, he urged, does not have to equal despair!

After Mark, Don stomped on to the stage in specially made boots which contained his toeless feet. His fine tenor voice captivated everyone as he sang, 'Oh how I love him, how I adore him...the great Creator became my Saviour...' He made eloquent gestures with his almost fingerless hands as he used his entire body as an expressive part of his singing. My eyes started to rove over the attentive audience. Suddenly

my heart skipped a beat as I spotted a familiar face—
Larry Cox! I couldn't believe my eyes. Larry was
obviously experiencing a change of attitude. The
bitterness and hostility once reflected in his face was
now replaced by deep thought as he leaned forward in
his chair, listening intently. I prayed for him and
for others like him in the audience who desperately
needed God. The evening closed with a forthright
message from New Zealand evangelist, Barry Reed. He
had contracted polio early in life, which had left his
legs withered and parts of his body deformed—but it
hadn't affected his strong faith and ability to preach
dynamically. Because of his own disability he understood only too well the temptations, frustrations and
hurdles faced by disabled people.

Barry certainly didn't mince words. 'It's a terrible
thing to go through life with a twisted body,' he said.
'It's a terrible thing to go through life with eyes that
cannot see the beauties of this world. But there's
something far more terrible—and that is going out into
all eternity blind—spiritually!'

He lowered his voice. 'There are disabled people
who, day after day, go through the steady grind of just
having to exist for another day. Nobody knows what
it's like not to be able to do things for yourself except
the person who's suffering it. But don't let your life
narrow itself down in the daily grind as to how you are
going to keep going. Let your life come free in Jesus,'
he pleaded. 'Don't excuse yourself because you are
disabled. '

'The God I serve wouldn't leave one of you out. It's
the individual who leaves God out of his or her life.
God knows about your secret longings to be a better
person...about your tears in the night...the lonely
hours as the dawning of the morning approaches. He
knows how you hate having to ask people to do things
for you.'

I sensed him deliberately pointing the message to a

climax, and I sat, heart pounding, wondering how he would conclude.

'I don't care what denomination you attend—Baptist, Methodist, Presbyterian, Anglican or Catholic—all must come to Christ the same way! And when the Spirit of God comes upon a person, he can transorm that sinner into a saint. He can make this people a great army.'

I absorbed his message. God could raise the disabled to become part of his great army, once they had caught that vision for themselves it would give them a new sense of purpose. It might mean financial sacrifice as they were challenged not to pour their energies and talents into something that is temporal and ultimately worthless. But it would give them an exciting life as they worked to build up the kingdom of God.

Barry's voice cut across my thoughts. 'You say, "The world is too strong. I can't resist all the temptations!" The Bible says, "Greater is he that is in you than he that is in the world." Your excuse is, "I might fail." Jesus said, "I will never leave you nor forsake you!"'

And then he reached the crux of his message. 'The greatest treasure we possess is ourselves. Surrender to God all you've got.'

Several moments ticked by. Then came the sound of a power chair moving as the occupant slowly made her way to the front. More sounds of movement followed. People in wheelchairs, people on crutches, people led by their 'seeing-eye' helpers.

Then it happened! Larry was moving his power chair out. Which way would he turn? To the back to escape, or to the front? I sat holding my breath. I felt the hair stand up on the back of my neck as I prayed. I agonised. And waited. Then, with his jaw set as though afraid that if he hesitated he might change his mind, he powered himself into line with the others already making their commitments to Christ at the altar.

Our eyes met. Gone was the hostility, the bitterness. From that time onwards, Larry became a new creation in Christ, a brand new man.

I bowed my head and praised God. And wept. The vision was now being fulfilled in the lives of my disabled friends.

Carried along on a wave of excitement, the obvious question was, 'Lord, what next?'

'A boat trip!' was his astounding reply. This and other activities introduced the disabled to a big world which many of them had never experienced.

As we waited on the wharf, the sun danced on the deep, greeny-blue waters. It was a glorious summer's day. Helpers carried heavy picnic hampers, filled with precooked barbecued sausages, bread rolls, club sandwiches, cakes and a variety of fresh fruits.

Once lunch was safely across the gang-plank, next came the stupendous feat of manhandling forty-two people in wheelchairs down from the quay and on to the ferry. It was a super-human task.

Amazingly, all that found its way overboard was one white walking cane, although one helper quickly discovered never to grab a wheelchair by the armrests because they automatically lift off! Fortunately the other five helpers had the wheelchair in hand, plus its occupant firmly held, otherwise there could have been a disaster!

Activities like this were a logistical nightmare, but our confidence grew as we became involved in all types of recreational and social pursuits from horse riding to floor hockey, wheelchair square dancing or hikes (more like rolls) through the bush.

All were 'firsts' for many of our disabled people, and they showed great tenacity and courage in undertaking such challenges.

An essential aim of our ministry was to enable the disabled to discover their special abilities in drama, music, sharing their faith, art and countless other avenues, allowing the Spirit of God to work both in and through them.

After the raising of Lazarus, who was somehow drawn out of the tomb still wrapped in grave clothes, Jesus turned to his friends and said, 'Loose him and let him go!' Jesus gave life, but the friends had the responsibility of releasing and unleashing that life.

Similarly, we sensed that it was our affirmations and encouragement, our provision of opportunities and setting of practical goals, that would unloose our disabled people and bring wholeness and freedom.

We pushed hard for the disabled to achieve greater goals, to be accepted and loved by the church, not just tolerated. We wanted them to be given opportunities to serve within the church for their spiritual gifts would add depth and richness to the body of Christ.

Those frantic years of pioneering required much time, patience and donkey work. I found that being called to pioneer meant both aloneness and loneliness. Aloneness because forging and fulfilling a vision involves ploughing new ground. Loneliness because there is no existing model, so one is separated in a real sense until the vision is sufficiently flushed out for others to see what it's all about.

I wanted so much to offer the best to my disabled friends. For each person was unique and faced his own set of unique challenges. But sometimes I became so bogged down in letter-writing, meetings, endless planning and the responsibility of keeping the vision before our members, that I overlooked showing God's love in a very simple way to a needy person.

On one occasion, when the going seemed particularly tough, I heard the voice of God whisper, 'If you can't find the time and energy to do the job properly after the sacrifices people have made for you, then don't do it at all!' I was devastated as I saw my wrong motives and my sometimes halfhearted commitment. If I emphasised excellence in the work of CFFD, then it was up to me to set an example.

But the greatest achievements were in the future. The finest lives were yet to be lived. The best books yet to be written. The most powerful sermons yet to be preached. The most comprehensive plans for missions and seminars within Christian Fellowship for Disabled were yet to be conceived.

Temptations often occurred to sidetrack us from the call of God. Often at our most vulnerable time the Enemy would present an appealing alternative.

One such lure was a request for me to become the President of a prominent (secular) organisation in Auckland associated with the needs of the disabled. It was an influential position, a very attractive alternative to staying with CFFD and all its struggles and demands.

The decision was agonising—to go where success looked immediate, or to remain true to the vision God had given, a vision that was being established with painstaking slowness.

Positioned at the crossroads of indecision, I searched for advice from someone whose impartial counsel I trusted—Sister Joy. She sensed I was standing at the crossroads and needed direct revelation from God in making the right decision. In her usual way, she paced back and forth across the room, deep in conversation with God.

Suddenly she whirled towards me. 'Margie,' her faced beamed with smiles and excitement, 'I see doors, many doors before you, doors on to platforms. No hands are used to open these doors—the wheels of your chair push them open. Without your chair they remain closed. Those doors represent your ministry. No one and nothing else can open those doors except your chair! Sitting in your chair you are in the centre of God's will. Be encouraged, he delights in you, Margie...there's so much more ahead for you...the best is yet to be!'

Through her prophetic words, I sensed again the call of God to a ministry which was in direct contrast to all the glamour and partying that the presidency offered. There was no denying where I would remain —in the perfect will of God. One division had been overcome. But there were more.

Di and I were close, so close in fact that sometimes I felt extremely threatened by her. We were often reminded of the sisters Mary and Martha in the Bible. Both loved Jesus, but both had different roles to perform. Through this period I learned an invaluable principle: If God has something for you, he will give it to you. You don't have to strive, and you don't have to be jealous about another person's recognition. God loves variety. We have been created individually, each with our own special gifts, but also with our own special limitations.

Disabled people often feel inferior and threatened in comparison with the superior abilities of the able-bodied. But God wants us to concentrate on the abilities we have, and to stop hankering for what we don't have. For myself, this is a process which still requires working through.

Throughout those early, whirlwind days, Hugh and Di committed themselves solely to the ministry. They showed no favouritism. Each person was special. God gave me the vision to establish the ministry, but it took steadfast commitment from Hugh and Di and a host of other willing and dedicated people to bring that vision to fruition.

As we worked together, our membership escalated to between 300 and 400 in the Auckland province.

The publication of our bimonthly magazine ignited interest throughout the land and we received requests from different areas for permission to establish local branches. The result was phenomenal growth, as CFFD branches began mushrooming in both New Zealand's North and South Islands.

Printing numbers leapt from forty in 1978 to 200 in 1979, 600 in 1981, to 2,000 in 1983. (Today several thousand are printed and distributed, not just throughout New Zealand but right across the globe.)

I likened the fellowship to an eagle's nest filled with young birds. To discover themselves truly they would eventually have to be pushed out of the nest. The executive committee, like the mother eagle, had oversight, knowing the importance of preparation and the timing for release. We constantly needed to listen to God's voice as to the timing of the release for the disabled so that they could step out in faith into utilising their unique giftings and talents.

We began to trust God for opportunities for teams to minister in churches of all denominations—disabled people themselves sharing their testimonies, a musical item, a poem or even preach a sermon. Thus a new phase of ministry opened as we inspired and challenged churches to take up the vision. As a result, many disabled people now found purpose and new meaning to life within their own churches.

One of the most difficult hurdles which confronted us in our increasing contacts with the disabled concerned sexuality. Immorality in the form of sexual therapy was being endorsed and encouraged within some institutions. The situation was complex, involving both staff and the disabled.

We were alerted to this problem as a result of counselling young women who felt overwhelmed by guilt because of sexual activity and often a resultant abortion.

Our response was to show God's love by supporting and affirming these girls, praying with them individually until they could forgive themselves and receive God's restoration and healing. We didn't want to be kill-joys, but we had to look honestly at God's standards on such issues as sexuality and fantasy. We couldn't use our disabilities as an excuse for compromise. Outside

God's rules, sexual activity only produces heartache, guilt, loneliness and eventually destruction.

A problem for many disabled people, especially those who can't hold positions of employment, is that they have too much idle time on their hands. It's easy to fall into the trap of fantasising about things. As the saying goes, 'Sow a thought, reap an action, reap an action, you reap a destiny.' So many people learn that lesson the hard way. We tried to encourage the disabled to reflect on the word of God, and develop good friendships with people who love the ways of God.

How does one cope with being disabled and single? Can one find fulfilment and be happy in accepting this as the will of God? What about sexuality? And fantasy? Is it a sin to be unhappy in the will of God? All nitty-gritty issues with which disabled people struggle.

We tried to encourage disabled people to hunger for God to lead them to a maturity and holiness of life, for that is our ultimate goal. However, it can be painful to live a life that is pleasing to God, and the disabled need enormous support in the midst of their pain. Marriage and all its pleasures is something every single person grapples with once in a while. It's natural, and only human!

As a fellowship we longed for a touch of God that would not just bring an invasion of power, but an invasion of purity into our midst. I understood the loneliness, the frustration and the isolation disabled people faced, I too faced the possibility of never having a man to hold and love me. Commitment to purity, I learned, needs to be restated day after day.

Many times Di and I talked into the small hours of the morning as we thought about how to meet the real depth of people's needs. What programmes and seminars could help answer the searching questions among our disabled people? And where was the power? Many were receiving ministry yet remaining unchanged. Too many broken hearts were not being healed. Lives were still bound and shackled. Our ministry was only touching the tip of an iceberg.

'Lord,' I found myself praying, 'there's got to be a stronger force. Let us powerfully penetrate both the world and the church.'

My mind flashed back to the television programme in which Kathryn Kuhlman interviewed Stan Mooneyham during the Vietnam War. I remembered the thousands of dollars donated to the hospital for disabled children—providing wheelchairs, crutches and trolleys for spina bifidas. 'This is love, giving them what they need,' she had said. 'Love talked about is easily turned aside, but love demonstrated is irresistible.'

We realised that love had to be the motivating force in our lives as Christians in a caring organisation. The supernatural love of God had given Jesus Christ to this world—and it was the supernatural love of God which would translate our words and actions into life and healing for our disabled people. But how could we really achieve this? How could we teach the disabled to love themselves when many had little or no self-worth?

The story of one young girl came to mind. It was set early this century, and centred around a girl who had lost her mind. She had an appalling background and her life just fell to pieces. As a result she became like an animal. When placed in an institution they put her in a cage and left her to rot.

However, within the institution there was a cleaning lady who would daily come to the iron bars of her cage. Using her broom handle she would push a tray of food through the bars and across to the girl. Then she'd fish around in the darkened cage until she found the girl and began to stoke her with the broom handle. This became a daily ritual. The days grew into weeks and the weeks to months.

Then a miracle happened. Slowly but surely the girl

recovered her mind as this cleaning lady ministered 'love' through her broom handle. The greatest force in all the universe penetrated through the broom handle into the girl, bringing healing and restoration.

One day the superintendent of that institution received a letter from the superintendent of another institution with this request: 'We have a girl who is terribly, terribly handicapped physically. Do you have someone who could come alongside her and give help and hope?'

The superintendent exclaimed, 'Yes, we do!' And he sent an attractive young woman, now of sound mind, who had once lain in a cage while a cleaning lady reached out to her with a broom handle. Her name was Anne Sullivan, and she became the life-long friend, teacher and nurse of Helen Keller. And all because of the love of God and a broom handle.

I reflected on that cleaning lady. She probably felt she couldn't do much for God. She probably wasn't a great preacher. She never saw the people to whom she ministered. But she poked her broom handle through bars and touched someone's life.

The love of God is a dynamic force, a force to be reckoned with. Christians must never underestimate the power of love.

Some of our disabled people were in similiar situations to Anne Sullivan. Yet where were our broom handles? Where was that dimension of love in our ministry? Why were we holding back in certain areas?

Then it dawned on me. Wasn't it my responsibility to encourage that dimension of love within the fellowship —to expect it from our executives, helpers and contributors? First and foremost, I must exhibit such love myself. But, I pondered, what was my broom handle? Again, what was my motive for showing the love of God?

'God, there are so many hopeless situations!' I cried, overwhelmed by the enormity of it all. 'There are so many desperate people who live in the pit of despair.'

'There are no hopeless situations, only people who've grown hopeless about them!' God's voice came back. 'In the world's eyes you too were junk which nobody knew what to do with. But I gave you people who loved you, who believed for you. I took a nobody and made her a somebody—don't ever forget that... but I'm not finished with you yet!'

In the months that followed, God had his own ways of teaching me so much more about the power of love.

12

I Want a Man

Mustering my energy and concentrating hard on my enunciation so that the shop assistant would be able to understand my unique style of speech, I blurted out my request loud and clear: '*I—want—a—man!*'

As soon as the words were out I realised what a ridiculous statement I'd made. The shop assistant looked at me non-plussed and, treating me as if I were deaf, she responded in a loud voice: '*You want a man?*'

'*Don't we all?*' boomed a voice from nowhere, and chuckles followed. Blushing, I gestured awkwardly towards the china figurines and turned to Helen for help. But Helen was nowhere to be seen. In fact she was doubled over with hysterical laughter outside on the pavement. Several painful minutes ticked by before she was able to regain enough composure to come back into the shop and explain to the shop assistant that I had come in a few weeks earlier and bought a lady figurine and was now returning to buy the male partner. Sadly, the figurine had been sold so my set remained incomplete.

This experience vividly illustrated what I was going through myself. Here I was in my early thirties seeing marvellous things happen as God opened the doors of adventure, ministry and opportunity, for this 'woman of God'. However, the real woman was aching and unfulfilled in certain areas and, as I had declared loudly, I wanted a man.

I wasn't coping with celibacy. I wasn't secure in my single status. I was full of questions, emotions and prayers. I was no less of a woman than my mobile counterparts. Although late in my social development it was all in me and now coming strongly to the fore.

I wept at weddings, struggled to rejoice with friends who were marrying, and lay awake crying at night, longing to be held, cuddled, whispered to, loved intimately, to have my womanhood affirmed. Of course, I realised marriage wasn't all kiss and bliss, but I was a romantic at heart and I prayed for Mr Right to come and sweep me off my wheels.

I really enjoyed art, and had pursued it initially by having private tuition and then by attending art classes. For me, holding the brush was an art in itself, requiring the utmost concentration to control my involuntary movements in order to apply the paint to where it should be. I clenched a shorter version of an ordinary brush between my teeth and thus was able to master up, down and across strokes by moving my head. The patience of my art teacher coupled with my grit and determination developed with time into material suitable for producing as Christmas cards for the Crippled Children Society.

It was at one of my art classes that I first met Todd Munro. Todd was a manager of a family business, and a voluntary worker in a drop-in centre for alcoholics. He was thirty-five, with a mop of dark curly hair, a trim moustache, and endearing soft brown eyes. He seemed full of strength and energy, and was obviously a gifted artist, particularly enjoying sketches in ink and charcoal pictures. He drew his chair alongside mine and in a few brief moments I gained insight into his interests, discovering the sincerity of his faith and the similarity of our Christian backgrounds. Our rapport was relaxed and immediate, and our conversation ended with his suggestion, 'Margie, let's talk some more. Can I come to visit you sometime and help with transport, draw pictures and assist you with art? It would be a joy, a pleasure to help you.'

'Sure, come over anytime,' I invited, not really expecting he'd take me up on the invitation. But I was wrong.

Three days later, on a Saturday morning, the phone rang. 'Good morning, beautiful lady.' I could hear his voice crackling with laughter as he sensed my surprise. 'Beautiful day outside. I've got some free time. How would you like to go to the bush for a picnic? I'll do a little fishing and we can go boating.'

Did my mind work overtime! I saw it all: the sun sparkling on the water, swans and water lilies, and me being propelled across it by a gorgeous hunk of a guy! However, my response was hesitant, betraying my social immaturity. Guys had never asked me out. What did I say now?

'Let me take you out,' Todd coaxed. 'I want to make up for what other men have denied you.' Eventually his persistence and sincerity won through. Live or die, sink or swim, what had I to lose? I accepted his invitation.

As the day wore on, what had initially seemed an overbearing approach become more relaxed and natural. My wheelchair didn't get in the way and there was no pity or embarrassment in his manner. He treated me as he would have treated any woman he liked. He was strong but gentle, giving me assurance that I'd be fine and he'd not let anything happen to me. He made me feel attractive and feminine. Todd pushed my chair as far as he could along the trail. Then he spread out a blanket, helped me out of my chair, and we shared the picnic lunch he'd brought. It was no problem to him to hold my food, and I contentedly munched away too enchanted to notice that I was eating a sardine sandwich (I detest sardine sandwiches!)

This date was the beginning of many more in the weeks and months that followed. My knight in shining armour would arrive weekends, weekdays, whenever, armed with cards, gifts, flowers, chocolates and exotic perfume. Thus 'Maid Margie' began to find her emotions surfacing. Dreams occupied both my waking and sleeping hours; the elusive and impossible suddenly seemed tangible and possible. We boated, fished, walked, picnicked, dined, laughed, shopped, painted and drew together, enjoying one another in an easy and natural way. The childlike person I was began to blossom into a mature woman, more self-assured, more aware of being feminine. Todd drew out my femininity so positively that the change was not painful or awkward but pleasant and exciting.

One day, on the spur of the moment, we decided we'd go for a swim in a friend's pool A girlfriend stripped off my clothes, whipped me into a swimsuit and whisked my chair out to the side of the pool. Todd was already in the pool and so my body was lowered into his arms. As he held me all sorts of emotions bubbled to the surface, and I was both excited and scared. But Todd was never put off by the physical aspects of my handicaps. The wheelchair never bothered him, nor my speech and my awkward and sudden movements. We joked, played and provoked one another as we would have done had I not been disabled.

'It's scarey,' I confessed to Di, 'but I like it. God has brought someone into my life, someone who really cares for me. This is the will of God,' I reasoned with Di. 'I never thought I could be so happy with a man.' We both talked excitedly as I thought about Todd, our relationship together and what was God's will in it all.

I turned to the Bible for answers and prayed fervently. The Bible began to underline and confirm my dreams: 'Delight yourself in the Lord and he will give you the desires of your heart.'

'No good thing will the Lord withhold from those who walk uprightly.'

'There are three things too wonderful for me to understand, no four. How an eagle glides through the sky...the fourth the growth of love between a man and a girl.'

Everything seemed to be lining up: circumstances, God's word, my heart. Todd had captivated my heart, and I loved him. I was a woman like any other woman, and I didn't want to turn into an old maid and be left on the shelf.

Di chuckled. 'I long for you to be married, Marg, to be happy, to have your desires and dreams fulfilled. But don't read more into Scripture than there is,' she warned. 'Be careful. Please be careful. Guard against becoming too involved. Romance is complex. It's not just your will and God's will that need to line up, but Todd's will as well.'

But I wasn't listening. God was saying it, therefore that settled it.

Todd took me several times to the drop-in centre where he worked. One day I was invited to share my testimony. It was a strange scene. The smell of unwashed beery men, plus a few women, wafted around. One had three teeth, another none at all. They all had grubby clothing, and eyes that were beady or else vague and distant. They leered at me as I began to speak. I tried desperately to identify with them: They had their problems and I had mine. Sounding more confident than I felt, I launched in. The frog story was a big hit and barriers began to melt. I found it easier to share from my personal experience of hurts, fears and frustrations, telling of my struggles in America, of inner healings and my time at Bible college. As I spoke to them, I longed to comfort them with the fact that Christ identified with them. So I told them about Jesus who was born in a smelly stable, who knew what it was like to be hungry, lonely, without a place to call his own, abandoned by his closest friends and finally paralysed on a cross by sin—my sin and their sin. But he overcame, and we, through him, can overcome.

I was appalled to see so many shackled and burdened lives in that building. It struck me again that the most disabled person in the world is the person without Christ—the person with no eternal future. The message was all so real to that hopeless, ragged mob sitting around me. I had seen congregations moved to tears before, but to see tears streaming down these grimy, unlovely faces was incredible. Tears began to stream down my own cheeks too as the love of God permeated that building. People rushed forward to grab my hand, to thank me for giving them hope.

'Thank you for sharing, for challenging us from your personal overcoming,' said one. Dirty hands wanted to touch, to hug, to express love. Just being in the presence of these folk made my own struggles seem insignificant. My dress, simple and flowing, was such a contrast to their garb. I felt like a princess by comparison.

Then a woman approached me. She was the closest thing to a witch I had ever seen—the only thing missing was her broomstick. She stank! I tried not to balk. Suddenly she leaned forward in excitement. Grabbing my hands she rattled her words out: 'I've had a vision of Jesus today—a lovely vision of Jesus. You've taught me God is love. He's real.' Others echoed her.

Todd was beside my chair, overjoyed by the response. Proud of me, he reached down for my hand and squeezed it gently. My heart fluttered as it had a thousand times before in the last six months. We beamed at each other. My emotions were becoming like a runaway train careering down the tracks at full speed.

'I don't think you should get too serious with Todd,' Di urged me once again. 'You'll get hurt, Margie. I

know he really likes you and he's sincere, but he has
needs of his own—needs of good friendship. I know
he's good for you to be with and I can tell he really likes
you—there's a real fondness there—but love? I'm not
sure.'

Di was happily married and she wanted the same
happiness for me. We often talked about marriage and
even planned my wedding! Di was concerned because
months had gone by and there had been no mention
from Todd about lifetime commitment, no ring forthcoming. She suspected Todd was playing safe, secure
behind my chair with no intention of marrying me. As
time went on she became more and more annoyed with
the way he was playing ball with my emotions.

I wanted to know where our relationship was really
going, so I sought out Todd's mum. Todd's family had
accepted me, showing no opposition to our relationship, and by this time Mr and Mrs Munro were 'Mum
and Dad'. I arrived at their home one Saturday afternoon rather emotionally strung out. Mum Munro, a
very perceptive lady, discerned my agitation and drew
me aside into the kitchen.

'What's wrong, darling?' her voice was soft. 'Is there
something troubling you? Margie, tell me, is it Todd?
You can tell me absolutely anything. Be open with me,'
she invited, encouraging me to open my heart.

'It's just. . .I don't know where I stand with him. I
sense affection, real fondness—but that's as far as he's
prepared to commit himself.'

I searched Mum Munro's face, trying to read her
eyes, and swallowed deeply before naming my inner
fears. 'I resent his hiding behind my chair. He's using it
as a protection, a security. I'm too much of a woman to
be strung along emotionally.'

'I love the guy,' I finally confessed. 'I want to know
—am I his woman or not?'

Slowly she walked across the room her arms en-
circled my shoulders. 'Listen to me, Margie,' she spoke

reassuringly, 'I know for a fact that when Todd marries that girl will be you.' I stared at her speechless. I was amazed at her confidence in knowing her son's mind. I began to express reservations, but she interrupted, smiling. 'Believe me, I know my son, his feelings, his make up. He lives for you—to please you. You're good for him.'

I couldn't believe my ears—I floated on cloud nine. Suddenly she pulled back, her eyes clouded with concern. 'Of course, you know Todd was once in love with a very beautiful girl. Marriage was in the wind and preparations were being discussed for their wedding.' Mum Munro spoke slowly as if bewildered. 'The girl unexpectedly cut the ties—just quit and ran. She's now married a fine young man and has two children. I don't understand what went wrong. Todd clammed up about the whole episode. I simply don't know,' she concluded, her voice trailing off. She reached down and pecked a kiss on my cheek. 'Try to rest. Give him over to the Lord. Trust God to bring it all to pass.'

Trust God. Yes, I trusted God. Trusting myself, my emotions was another kettle of fish. I wanted Todd to open up to me and tell me where I stood. Did he love me or didn't he?

That evening we were dining together in a restaurant. Soft music played in the background. I wore one of the red roses Todd had bought me—he'd pinned it to my evening dress.

Candles illuminated the table and he took my hand and whispered, 'Can I be devoted to you for the rest of my life?'

I lowered my gaze—my eyes unable to meet his. What in the world do you mean, I wondered desperately. You're not asking me to marry you. If you were I'd say 'yes' without hesitation. You're not saying, 'I love you.' If you were I'd say, 'I love you,' back.

'Exactly what do you mean?' I demanded. 'Please make a stand.'

Slowly Todd filled me in on his previous love affair. It had shattered him and he had vowed that he would never again become deeply involved with a woman. He wanted love with no strings attached. Yes, his aim was to be my 'devoted friend' for the rest of his life, but he had no intention of marrying any woman unless God had other ideas—and God would need to speak very loudly and clearly about them.

Sensing my hurt, Todd closed both his hands over mine and waited. Slowly one hand moved and lifted my chin and tilted my head back. 'Look at me,' his voice was firm. 'It's not the end of the world. I need you. Many people have a close relationship without marrying—that too can be a rich and deep commitment and in the purposes of God.'

The food in my mouth had suddenly become tasteless and I wanted to spit it out. My heart felt as if it had been stabbed. Devoted friend? I was madly in love. Just friends? That was virtually impossible considering the way I felt about him. Maybe he just needed time to sort out his true feelings. I didn't dare impose, but finally I began to realise that Di and others were right. I was caught in a web of feelings, dreams and desires. Over the next few days I was to learn even more forcibly that I wasn't Todd's woman.

I'd always been intensely jealous when other pretty able-bodied women were around Todd and soon a conniving female challenged me to a duel. She was out to get Todd, she declared with confidence, and was going to use all her womanly wiles to do so. At first, Todd brushed it off, but I felt threatened, aware that there was no way I could compete. A real cat fight blew up between us. I went into overdrive—fretting, fuming and burning with envy. Todd was furious with my behaviour, and his interest in me dwindled. I learned that my opponent's womanly wiles had paid off and that she and Todd were dating. What a mess I was in. My happiness had led to envy, envy to hatred and

hatred to murder in my heart and possibly in the flesh
if I'd had the co-ordination to fire a bullet!

Di spent hours picking up the pieces. Just because I
was in a wheelchair didn't mean I was exempt from
being tried and tempted in the way other single women
are. I'd learned a lesson the hard way—never look at
any man with the idea that he is a potential husband.
It's good to have healthy male friendships, but not to
become caught up in a flood of emotion as I had done.

Finally I came to terms with things and was
honest with myself. I had not been realistic about the
relationship. It does take someone special to commit
themselves to a person in a chair for the rest of their
life.

Di continued to hang in with me, praying, encouraging and supporting. 'If an eagle's wings are tilted
downwards when a storm strikes it will be dashed to
pieces on the earth,' she said. 'But if its wings are tilted
upwards it will rise, making the storm bear it beyond its
fury. We need to be tilting upwards when things fall
apart in our lives. We need to soar through the storm.
Believe it, Margie, nothing is ever wasted. The Lord
will work it out for good. Let it go. You have the choice
to let this make you bitter or better. It's not so much
what the relationship has done to you, but what you
can learn from it.'

Saying goodbye wasn't easy. I ached; I was raw and
sore to the core. Hadn't Todd been the one who had
encouraged me by calling every night and taking me
out every weekend without fail? Hadn't he been
the one who took me to fancy restaurants, gazing
devotedly into my eyes and making half promises?

The breakthrough in the emotional turmoil came
when I was discussing the situation with a pastor
friend. 'Pick up the pieces,' he advised. 'Allow God to
put your life back together again. You've been playing
a game which able-bodied people play. They cope, and
so can you. Never enter into competition with another

woman, either in ministry or over a man. It's a foolish game which the immature play—it's not in keeping with the will of God.

'For sanity's sake,' he continued, 'Let's commit this to the Lord. Confess your folly. Die to yourself, your emotions and your fickle desires.' He picked up his well-thumbed Bible and turned to Genesis 22, the story of how God singled out the most precious thing in Abraham's life—his son—and asked for him as a sacrifice. God often starts his tests of character with the things we love the most. That day he was calling me to sacrifice my 'Isaac'—my desire to be married.

As I prayed, God did the rest. Suddenly I was free from all the inner conflict and turmoil. It was a painful experience, but my life and ministry were richer and deeper as a result.

13
The Conflict

Once Todd had transferred his affections, I threw myself into my ministry. This helped to keep the grey matter occupied, and didn't allow pride or pity to have any party with me. I was determined to fulfil the vision God had entrusted to me and this pursuit consumed me. Time doesn't heal—God does!

I was now living in a bedsitter in a family home in the surburbs of Auckland. Although I'm disabled, there's much I can do for myself, but I do need help with dressing, undressing and preparing food. In order to give the family household space and take a break myself, I would regularly spend the long summer holidays, December to February, with my parents in Te Puke, New Zealand's kiwi fruit capital. This is situated in a beautiful rural area, with beaches nearby. I looked forward to spending my summer vacations at home with my family.

Mother was an excellent cook and an active Christian, and was always inviting people to our home. One of her regular guests was Simon Peters. He was somewhat older than myself, stocky and strong-shouldered with a crop of curly blondish hair. His gentle blue eyes betrayed both his own hurt and his compassion for others who had been hurt. His wife of twenty-five years had recently left him to live with his best friend. In the midst of his despair he'd cried out to God, and God had responded and entered his life. The emotional and mental suffering Simon had experienced became the springboard for his sensitivity and compassion towards others—far more than he realised.

At first, I sat in the background when he called. We'd met on previous occasions as Simon had been one of the local shop owners. He'd seemed embarrassed when he had to serve me in his shop (in fact, he would avoid doing so if possible!). However, he was now slowly coming to understand my speech and coping with my awkward movements, and we began to relate and chat naturally.

It was 9 o'clock one morning. The sun was streaming in through the kitchen window, I was sitting at the table, my back to the outside door, engrossed in preparing a sermon. At the pad of footsteps I turned to see who was approaching.

'Good morning, good morning,' Simon greeted me cheerfully, standing in the doorway. I gestured with my arm, inviting him in and to pull up a chair. Mother always had a teapot, hot and ready on the table, for callers. Simon was now such a regular visitor that he was addicted to tea and was almost part of the family!

He glanced over, his eyes resting on the material I was preparing for my sermon. '"The purpose of suffering"—sounds heavy stuff,' he gibed. But I saw pain in his face, and sensed his aloneness and need of companionship.

He sighed as he reached across the table for the teapot and silently poured himself a cup. I waited, eager for the conversation to continue. He sipped his tea. His eyes glistened, betraying the fact that tears weren't far away.

'If only I had more faith...faith to handle life better, myself better, then maybe I'd have the answers for solving our matrimonial problems.' His voice sounded a little choked. He placed a cold drink in front of me and held a straw to my lips. Thoughtfully I sucked my orange juice, weighing up my words before I spoke—wanting to bring comfort.

'Simon, it's OK to hurt,' I said. He appeared relieved I'd given him permission to feel the way he did. 'Some people think that the Christian life is one roller-coaster ride; that nobody should ever have problems or ever be sick—and if they are they should be healed immediately. If money is required all they have to do is ask God and the heavens will open and down it pours. If people don't prosper then they are not spiritually on the ball!'

I swallowed, took another breath, then continued. 'Exaggeration maybe, but I find this kind of spirituality unrealistic. It isn't practical, it's not sensitive and it's definitely not love. In fact,' I added emphatically, 'it is not spiritual. It often brings condemnation on a person. That's not the work of the Holy Spirit.'

I stopped and looked intently at him, waiting to hear his thoughts. Although he didn't know it, he was about to give me the content of my sermon—from his own life.

He sat quietly for some time before saying, 'Scripture has taken on new depth and personal meaning for me recently. I've been reading about Job. He was someone of real moral and spiritual calibre. God said, "There's none like him!" That's some testimony!'

'What do you think God's ultimate purpose for Job was?' I probed, curious to sound Simon out.

Simon was thoughtful. 'God's aim was to prosper him—bless him doublefold. The trials and tests were to make Job twice as trustworthy. God's aim was to give him double portion out of his calamity, developing something more precious than would have ever developed if the devil had left him alone. In the beginning Job wasn't ready, so God had to allow him to be stripped so he could be rebuilt.'

'Interesting,' I murmured, eager to gain more insight. 'I guess God had to be willing many times to be misunderstood and misjudged.'

Simon chipped in. 'I believe God is willing to be misunderstood by those he's seeking to bless and those looking on. Job was tested in specific areas—first his crops, a financial area, then his sons and daughters, an emotional area, then everything apart from his wife was taken, leading to mental suffering. Then he endured physical pain when his body was covered in boils. I can just imagine him picking up a piece of plate to scrape himself with as he tried to gain some relief.'

'Then, to add to his misery, his not too sympathetic wife comes out and says, "Why don't you curse God and die?" She was so embarrassed by his situation that all she wanted was for him to get it over and done with.'

'I would say that was spiritual suffering. Yet, amidst utter chaos, Job bowed his head and worshipped. His declaration of faith was, "Should we accept good from God and not trial too?" In this situation, Job accepted everything that came to him as being from the hand of God.'

Simon spoke softly, yet with deep sincerity. 'That's maturity, Marg. I wish I could be like him. He was a man who trusted God no matter what. There are some things in this life that we will never understand. But be assured, dear lady, the trials of this earth are nothing compared to the triumphs of heaven.'

There was certainty in his voice. I could identify with all he was sharing. I pondered other biblical passages. Job had suffered, Jeremiah had suffered, Paul had been shipwrecked and imprisoned. Simon was suffering, but I knew it wouldn't be wasted. God would work it through for good.

As I turned to Simon, words tumbled out: 'I never cease to be amazed that when Christians encounter trials and testings they give the devil so much credit. That's wrong. Trial and testing often come from God to develop our own character, and to make us more responsible and sensitive.'

I was beginning to understand that few of God's people go through life without encountering their 'fiery trial' (1 Pet 4:12, Authorised Version). All of us encounter something, if not physical, then in other ways—financial, loss of loved ones, ridicule, divorce. So often our attitude is: 'Lord, I can do anything but that...go anywhere but there...do anything but this... Lord, I'm begging you, please don't let this happen to me.' How many times had my fears prompted such stipulations?

Without realising it then, I was about to have one of my legalistic, self-righteous views deeply challenged— and that concerned divorce. As a student at Faith Bible College one of our assignments was on the biblical view of divorce and remarriage. This is a highly complex and controversial subject. Various students were assigned live case studies about a situation where divorce and remarriage conflicted with pulpit ministry. Within my own group this provoked considerable contention. My fellow students expressed far more tolerance, but I was adamant that divorce and remarriage would bring reproach to the ministry—a stigma—and that a person would suffer the serious consequences of tampering with God's anointing. My passionate concern was to protect the purity of the ministry and the 'minister'.

In my opinion God hated divorce and a divorced Christian cannot remarry. So I was somewhat taken aback when our group leader indignantly responded to my rigidity.

'Margie, one day I hope you fall in love with someone who is divorced—and I hope it hurts!'

Simon and I talked in depth for hours during those summer holidays, sharing the word of God, what each of us had learned through our individual suffering, and how suffering had not demolished us but developed us.

We enjoyed many things and many times together:

feeding the ducks on the lake, watching a sunset, the restless crashing of the waves, meandering along the beach, picking wild flowers, throwing coins in the fountain, picnicking at local scenic spots and enjoying a peaceful bush walk. Simon would often read to me, as well. Some days he would stay for breakfast, lunch and tea. Eventually, he became my best friend.

It was February. The holidays over, the time came for me to return to Auckland and take up my responsibilities as President of Christian Fellowship for the Disabled. Ahead lay new goals and challenges for the new year's activities.

Our annual election of officers (in March) were approaching. Unexpectedly, my position came under heavy attack from another disabled person: an intelligent, highly qualified woman, she was determined to take over the leadership. During my absence many of the Fellowship had been canvassed and were supportive for her ideas for providing just a platform for the skilled and the educated. My credentials and education did not fall into these categories, I simply had a sense of God's calling. And those God calls he also enables. I depended upon this truth as the storm of conflict raged. But as she spat out her criticisms, I found my confidence being chipped away.

I was full of questions myself. I felt as if my whole being had been encased in stone to withstand what was happening. 'Let's pray,' Hugh and Di announced immediately. A day of prayer and fasting was held and we battled aggressively in the heavenlies, striving for unity and the retention of the original vision.

God spoke to us through Zechariah 'Don't think that I might change my mind...Here is your part; tell the truth. Be fair. Live at peace with everyone. Don't plot harm to others; don't swear that something is true when it isn't. How I hate that sort of thing!' says the Lord. God was exorting us not to be afraid or discouraged—the battle was his, not ours. I felt uncertain and inadequate and spent much time agonising before God about it all.

Simon had been a regular correspondent since my return to Auckland. He sensed my tension in my letters, and wrote back, encouraging me to stay centred in God's will. He prayed daily for the committee and the ministry of Christian Fellowship for Disabled and would often enclose a scripture, a little drawing or humorous cartoon in his letters.

The weekend before the dreaded election of officers, the phone rang. It was Simon. To my surprise and delight, he'd booked himself into a nearby motel. It was wonderful to relax in his company and know his support. And to leave the outcome of the meeting with the Lord.

Finally, election day came, and amazingly God over-ruled. During the selection process, there was no challenge to my leadership. It became clear that Satan had used this woman and her allies to undermine and oppose the work. It was near midnight when I returned to my room. A pile of mail was awaiting me on my bed. I was tired, very tired, but I couldn't resist sifting through the bundle of letters and hunting for Simon's. I knew it would be there, but I certainly wasn't expecting the contents to be what they were. Inside was a sketch plan of a house designed specifically for a wheelchair, and with it a proposal of marriage. I sat on my bed, utterly dumbfounded. If I read the contents of that letter once I read them six or seven times.

He couldn't mean he wanted to marry me. Sure, during the past three months a close bond had developed between us. Now he was my best friend. Sure I loved him, but with no strings attached. This time I'd been careful to keep the relationship on a platonic level. As I read the letter, I grew very angry. All this romantic nonsense would spoil our good friendship, driving a wedge between us. For me, the underlying issue was my views on divorce.

A whole gambit of thoughts came into my mind, as though a dam in my head had burst. What would my parents think? They held strong views that scriptural principles concerning the issue of divorce and remarriage had no loopholes. My friends and colleagues in CFFD—what would they think? Where did this begin? When had Simon started to care—and why?

Suddenly, I began to laugh. Why, marriage to Simon would mean I'd become wife, mother and grandmother all in one go, as four of Simon's five children were married and he had three grandchildren. That sure would make me grow up fast! I was in stitches. Ridiculous, absurd, out of the question. The guy was crazy, totally unrealistic, grabbing at straws.

My emotions sea-sawed with my thoughts. Part of me was angry, yet another part yearned to be loved. I was elated with the feeling that me, a wheelchair woman, had won someone's affection all fair and square. There was a measure of healing in just knowing he loved *me*! My problem was how to progress from here without losing my friend.

In the early hours of the morning I resolved to work things through by writing and giving a definite 'no'. So next day, I positioned myself at the typewriter and, with the aid of my mouthpiece, I pecked out a letter endeavouring to nip things in the bud.

I felt concerned for my parents, as by now Simon was a part of our family and their good friend. I didn't want to cause a rift between them, so at the earliest opportunity I planned to discuss the matter with them.

It wasn't long before the opportunity of going home for a weekend came. Mother was quietly knitting and no one else was around, so I braved it. Taking a deep breath, I announced to Mother that I had something I wanted to talk with her about, and would she please not react. She looked up from her knitting and calmly waited for me to proceed.

'Simon's asked me to marry him!' I announced.

To my astonishment, I found Mother had known for some time about Simon's depth of feeling towards me and had sensed that things had developed.

'Well, what do you think?' I quizzed.

'He's a gift—a real gift. Love like Simon has for you comes only once in a lifetime, Marg. A younger man would never cope. I know he can and would.'

I stared, speechless.

'You'd be a fool to spurn his love,' she persisted.

'But I don't love him,' I retorted. 'A friendship, yes, but lovers, no!'

Mother threw the ball back in my court. It was my problem and I was responsible. As far as she was concerned Simon was an answer to prayer. Should anything happen to her she had the utmost confidence that Simon would be ideal for me. Her answer was unexpected and somewhat confusing, opposed to the response I'd received from close friends: 'Margie, please don't marry him—divorce, remarriage and ministry don't mix.'

Why couldn't he be God's guy for me? Why was it that every man who came into my life posed a problem? I always fell in love with men who didn't want a woman in a chair, and now the boot was on the other foot. I was loved by a man whom I considered to be the wrong one. My Brethren Pentecostal indoctrination on the issue of divorce and remarriage was deeply inbedded within me, and books I'd read and teaching I'd been exposed to reinforced this absolute conviction.

Before me I had an open door—ministry. I was driven to fulfil the vision God had given me, and for me there was a clear-cut division—marriage or ministry. I didn't feel I had the energy to cope with both.

The CFFD Easter camp was approaching and I encouraged Simon to enlist as a helper. Part of me wanted indirectly to deter him, and I saw camp as an opportunity to do so. He could cope with one disabled person, but how would he cope with a whole group of disabled people together imposing their needs upon him all the time?

Simon accepted the challenge and was assigned to a spastic guy—a teenager who required help when bathed, dressed and toileted.

Meal time was my test time, and I positioned myself across the dining hall in a strategic spot so I could watch his reactions. Our food arrived at the table, and immediately the disabled began to pick up their cutlery. The majority insisted on feeding themselves. Saliva, mixed with gravy and vegetables, dribbled down their chins. Some plates began to swim with it, and heads were thrown back as they chewed with their mouths open, bits of food flying everywhere.

My own stomach began to churn, and I looked away. Simon didn't balk at all. He sat patiently feeding a severely handicapped lady, then a severely disabled man. That weekend he wheeled chairs on bush hikes, toileted men, washed soiled underwear, made beds, showered people. Nothing dampened his enthusiasm. He did anything and everything; where he could be 'hands' for someone disabled he was. He was the epitome of love in action.

He was appointed a group leader, responsible for developing discussions in small groups. Armed with a pile of study books he worked hard at digging out material and involving each member in the discussion.

Our camp chairman was impressed by his devotion. 'What a lovely fellow, Margie. He's so committed', he told me with a quizzical grin.

As the weekend progressed, so did my admiration for Simon. No one was too much bother. He showed love, compassion and acceptance to all with whom he had contact.

'Besides, sweetheart,' he smiled, encircling his arm around my shoulder and looking tenderly into my face, 'you're a piece of cake compared with some of these precious gems. Helping you is a delight.' The guy was impossible—there was no deterring him.

We drove home from camp, tired but happy. The leaves were beginning to turn gold on this beautiful autumn morning, and the lake sparkled. I was suddenly nervous in this romantic setting. It was the first time we'd been alone since Simon's marriage proposal. We needed to talk—I wanted his friendship.

'I'm going to take all day to drive you home so I can be with you,' Simon murmured quietly. He was even more nervous than I was. But as the miles passed our awkwardness melted and we began to talk openly.

Our discussion was about a friend I worried about. Judy was in her early thirties and had recently become engaged to a non-Christian guy. She had become desperate about marriage, not wanting to be left on the shelf.

'So you feel she's grabbing at straws,' queried Simon.

'Amazing,' I hinted. 'how lonely people desperately grab at straws.'

Simon took my point and slowed down the car. Leaning towards me he reached for my hand. 'Darling, I wouldn't waste my time grabbing at straws. I love you, really love you. Don't you realise how much?'

I knew then that he loved me, loved me deeply, and he was not about to play with my emotions. I could see he was finding it difficult being around me and having his love spurned.

'Simon, you are impossible!' I exploded, not wanting him to continue expressing his love. 'This is utterly ridiculous. I have never encouraged you with romantic nonsense. Have you seriously thought about the pressures and frustrations financially, emotionally—sexually, in marrying a severely disabled woman?'

I took a deep breath. 'I could never be happy or fulfilled not being able to serve you fully sexually. I'd be beside myself with frustration if I weren't able to express love and tenderness fully as a woman.'

My mind flicked back to the sessions at various rehabilitation centres by doctors on the possibility of love-making and on being able to have children.

Simon remained resolute, undeterred. If God was in our relationship, God would work this area of marriage through. Nothing would deter his love.

'But Simon, I'm severely handicapped.'

'But something overlooks all that.'

'What?'

'Love!'

So the stage was set. Over the following months Simon did all he could to woo and win my love. Often he'd arrive from nowhere at different parts of the country where I would be speaking. Church service after church service, CFFD activity after CFFD activity, he'd be there for me, waiting patiently in the background. Through it all I watched his affection for me deepen. Every time I sensed his feelings increase, I double-checked mine. What do I feel? Where are we going?

And the inevitable happened. Something I'd never expected—I loved him, loved him deeply. Yet I was not willing to be honest about my feelings. Inwardly I struggled. His love had worn me down.

'I love the real you, the person inside,' he often said. She's not disabled. The body is, but not the real you.'

I responded to his love and tenderness. I enjoyed feeling him next to me. My personality came alive in his presence, and my mind was stimulated by our rapport.

It was late one Sunday afternoon. Simon strode across the room with a red rose extended to me. 'Smells nice, doesn't it?' he winked. 'Here, let me put it in water for you.'

He disappeared into the kitchen, returning seconds later with a vase.

Setting it on my desk, he walked across the room, picked me out of my chair and held me in his arms. He brushed his lips across my mouth and carried me into the living room to the couch. Jippy, our much-loved family dog, scrambled out of the way. It was good to be home in front of the fire. I'd just arrived home from taking church services with other members from CFFD. Two teams had been ministering in the Bay of Plenty area. The schedule was hectic. I was tired. Too tired and too vulnerable. I began to think how much I loved being home—with a cosy fire, with Jippy curled up at the end of the couch. And with Simon.

Simon's close whispers interrupted my thoughts. 'I love being with you, looking after you.'

'I lay my head on his shoulder. Silence fell. 'You look exhausted,' he murmured as his lips touched my cheek. 'I could see speaking was a real effort today.'

It had been my sixth speaking engagement that week and the pace and emotional output were taking their toll.

Simon rose and threw another log onto the fire, then came back and sat close to me. I nestled my head on his shoulder once more, moving my body into the cradle of his arm. I dared not look at his face, but I knew he was looking at me. He was silent for a moment and I wondered at his strength, his tenderness, drawing me to him. I knew better, so why did I respond? His lips touched my forehead; I tilted my head back inviting his kiss. The moment was warm. He held me close, pressing his cheek against mine, and stroked my hair from my forehead. I sensed God near, so near we could have touched him!

Time stood still. 'It would work,' Simon whispered tenderly. 'You feel so right in my arms! Marry me, Marg, please. I've worked it through, prayed fervently. We can do it.'

I'd never imagined anyone loving me this much. I wanted to be loved, but other words cascaded through my mind: 'You marry him and you won't have a ministry...divorce and remarriage don't mix...that relationship will rob you of your anointing...'

'Please, Margie, don't marry him,' close friends had cried. I was walking through my 'fiery trial'—divorced man versus ministry. We were talking about a very important commitment.

Suddenly I pulled myself out of his arms, moving away. I felt like a yo-yo—my mind, my emotions, my physical desires were taking me from heaven to hell, from hope to hopelessness, from fulfilment to barrenness. I was torn between two worlds—man or ministry —and there was no overlap.

The compelling force was the call of God on my life. I knew my life wasn't my own. It was wrong to be leading him on. One of us was going to be hurt, deeply hurt. I was very afraid—afraid of losing him, not just in the romantic sense but as a friend. I was being cruel and I loathed myself for it.

Simon's eyes reflected the fire and I saw his tears. 'Marg, I just can't go on being close, spending more and more time with you. I'm finding it too hard. Either you marry me or we break up and never be close again ...I can't imagine not being close to you.' His voice was broken. 'But if this is what you feel about your ministry, then we are going to have to break up.' The words tumbled out.

I was faced with a choice: would it be man, or would it be ministry? I dissolved into a flood of tears. Simon knew from my response that my choice was ministry.

'You won't see me again?' I choked through sobs.

He shook his head. 'No,' he said firmly, then reaching across the couch he scooped me up into his arms and carried me across to my wheelchair. Seating me securely, he left the room. When he returned he was carrying the handcrafted pulpit he'd designed to fit my wheelchair. Dumping it on the floor beside me, he spat out the words: 'Ministry it is then,' and he turned his back and walked out.

No one will ever know the pain and the turmoil I suffered dying to that love. I loved him more than life itself. For a time I loved him more than God. I didn't want to miss the excitement of living with a man.

But God hadn't released me from my original call. The heartache was great. Yet finally I came to a place in my life where I was willing to give up everything, even Simon, and die.

I bowed my head and said it out loud: 'Lord, I surrender all. Take my body, my heart—all are yours.'

14

Courageous Faith

Faithful are those who have visions and are willing to pay the price to see them become reality! Faithfulness to Christ can be costly. It may involve being misunderstood by close friends, colleagues in ministry, and sometimes family members. It also involves constant attack from an Enemy subtly disguised within the ranks.

Faithfulness to Christ can cost people their home, their sweetheart, their dreams, their passions and ambitions—and sometimes their own lives. Often they do not see the results of their labours, for the seeds they have sown bring forth fruit in varying seasons—sometimes after their life itself has finished. A full reward will not come until after the work is completed.

Serving the Lord is a great challenge, and no other life offers greater rewards. I had accepted that challenge.

God allowed much refining to occur during the fiery trial of my romance with Simon. I had matured as a woman, and grown in sensitivity and compassion. I was more complete in myself, having known the release and response of love. My changed character bore witness to the truth: 'It's better to have loved and lost than never to have loved at all.'

This refining brought me to a place where God could entrust me with the responsibility and privilege of investing in lives for him. What price can be put on a person's life? There's no trouble too great. There's no humiliation too deep. There's no love too strong. There's no labour too hard. There's no expense too large. It is worth it if it is spent in winning one person to Jesus Christ!

Faithfulness to Christ is a walk of adventure. We go from strength to strength as we go from struggle to struggle, and challenge to challenge. For me, this discovery became the gateway into new dimensions in my relationship with God. I had learned that if I looked after the depth of my relationship with God, then he'd look after the breadth of my ministry. For anyone contemplating service for the Lord, there must be a time of preparation before performance. A vital lesson is learning to sit before God. God is not interested merely in our activity—he's interested in us spending time on our knees, receiving our plans from heaven and not our own fund of good ideas.

After my traumatic farewell with Simon, I needed time alone to think, to pray, to be with God. As I surrendered my life afresh to him, he came and gave me another vision of myself, whole and healed, wearing the yellow dress, white shoes and pearl necklace. This time I stood at heaven's doors with the Master alongside me.

It was the day of reckoning. People gathered, waiting before the Master to present to him their life's work. Various members from CFFD began arriving and I noted with interest and a certain degree of pride that many of them were people I had encouraged and helped to develop and utilise their talents and abilities.

The first such person to present himself before Jesus was a man disabled both by polio and cancer. I knew him well.

'Welcome!' greeted the Lord. Then he enquired, 'What is in your hands?'

The man slowly opened his tightly clenched fingers

to reveal ten…twenty…thirty magnificent gold coins. I knew immediately that those coins were symbols, representing his giftings and talents, developed and produced through his life. And CFFD was a vital factor in their formation.

'Well done, good and faithful servant!' pronounced the Master. 'Enter into the joy of your reward!'

The man beamed, ecstatic with the reward of dedicated service under the most horrific physical conditions.

That wasn't all. As the Master stooped to gather the talents from his hands their fingers touched and an immediate physical wholeness spread like lightning through his entire body; every joint unlocking, every muscle restored, withered limbs filling out, disease fleeing. Everything made new.

The two of us danced together. We laughed, we cried, we waltzed around. The wonder of co-ordinated hands, perfect speech and functioning legs and arms! We were free—so free!

Then in the twinkling of an eye, the scene changed. My moment of accountability had come. The Master beckoned me forward. He stood quietly with his hands outstretched, waiting to receive my contributions— my bright gold coins. As I placed these in the palms of his hands, I recoiled, shocked. Across the face of each coin, damning words appeared: lovelessness, jealousy, half-heartedness, criticism, wrong motives, bitterness, unforgiveness, sensuality, selfishness. I watched in anguish and shame as the bright coins were tarnished by the writing and turned black.

The Master's eyes were like fire, consuming what I had believed were beautiful, acceptable talents of quality. He'd weighed my works in the balance and found them wanting.

'They cost so much,' I choked, my eyes fixed on those ugly black coins.

'Tell me, what do you really understand about cost?'

the Master queried, gently displaying his two nail-
pierced hands.

Fresh understanding slowly dawned. In that sacred
moment I realised that the Master was challenging me,
calling me to deepen my relationship with him and to
rise to new levels of discovery and commitment. I must
let go of introspection and binding fears, and stop
focusing on the past. I must move forward.

It was vital for me to have this vision of God's
glory and holiness before I could understand what he
wanted to show me about the hidden sins which
brought reproach to him and his work. As I stood
transparent before the Master, two scriptures burned
deep within me. 'If we endure, we will also reign with
him' (2 Tim 2:12); 'We are heirs...if indeed we share
in his sufferings in order that we may also share in his
glory' (Rom 8:17).

I eagerly desired to share in his glory, yet I ran hard
from the fellowship of his sufferings. Suffering, however, is an integral part of ministry. This came as a
revelation: *No suffering—no sonship. No suffering—no
reigning.*

'I don't like it!' I cried, 'but I want it. Lord, you can
do anything!'

Then I glanced down in amazement. My clothing
was now a brilliant white and in my hand I held an
exquisite medallion. I stared at it, awestruck. It was
made of pure gold, studded with precious, glittering
jewels—diamonds, rubies, sapphires and emeralds—
the hallmark of royalty.

The Master had found this one talent in me, regardless of my flaws and imperfections, and produced
something of incredible value.

With authority he declared: 'I demand a quality of
life from you with excellence...'

Quietly he turned with outstretched arms towards
the crowd that had gathered from the fellowship and
ushered them towards two huge marble-like doors. At

his command the doors rolled back. Though I was never permitted to enter through these, I watched with baited breath as one of my disabled friends enthusiastically raced ahead to enter a huge celestial hallway. She called back to me, her face transfigured by beauty, her body now perfect, her spirit and voice lilting.

'Margie, believe me,' she gasped, 'the half has not been told. It's going to be worth it all. Hang in there. God's got greater things ahead!' She vanished, leaving those words ringing in my ears.

Several months lapsed. In late November 1980 I accepted an invitation to speak at a drop-in centre which catered for single parents and alcoholics, and others suffering hurts and loneliness.

The building was crammed to capacity, and as I glanced about I realised I was at home on their turf. I understood their heartaches, their feelings of rejection and frustration. Yet compared to what many of these folk had endured, my suffering was minimal. Hurting people don't care how much you know until they know how much you care. They want someone to understand their pain; someone to love them and to accept them as they are.

All around me were people with real needs. In myself, I had nothing to give them except my love, and my experiences that when life handed me lemons, God could teach me how to make lemonade.

I believe in being real with people, and so that day I shared my own ups and downs, my failures, my questionings. And my discoveries. The essence of life, I said, was relationships—the reality of our relationship with our Creator and the reality of our relationships with others. Each requires honesty, commitment and humility, and there is often pain as they are worked through.

I will never forget the sense of joy and purpose I felt as God used my life that day to touch theirs with a measure of healing, giving freedom of mind and spirit. After the meeting people milled around my chair. Some just wanted to talk. Others requested prayer. Still others wanted to reach out and touch me to show their love.

As they expressed themselves in their individual ways a woman whom I didn't know placed a card on my lap. I glanced down at it and its words gripped me. Printed in ink was a verse which read: 'I have set before you an open door.' I mulled over that little verse for days, trying to fathom out what God was saying to me. My search of the Scriptures uncovered more. The verse read: 'I know thy works...I have set before you an open door, and no man can shut it; you have little strength, yet you have kept my words and not denied my name. Invitations to speak began rolling in, spurred on by the forthcoming International Year of Disabled Persons. This was to be my 'open door', providing platforms from which I would share my story to people in our nation.

I felt nervous and inadequate, totally out of my depth. Yet in my pursuit for wisdom and direction, I felt I should read the Book of Judges. As I read chapter 6 on the call of Gideon, I found that my questions echoed his. I took heart from the discovery that when we think we can't—then God can!

Israel had been under virtual siege by the Midianites for seven weary years. Gideon was threshing wheat— crouching in a winepress to avoid detection by the enemy—when an angel appeared with a message. 'The Lord is with you, mighty warrior' (Judg 6:12).

I chuckled. I could almost visualise Gideon's head popping up out of the winepress: 'Were you talking to me?' He'd probably been called a lot of things during his lifetime, but never that. 'The Lord turned to him and said, "Go in the strength you have and save Israel out of Midian's hand. Am I not sending you?"' (6:14).

Gideon reminded the angel that he was the weakest

member of the weakest clan of the weakest tribe in the weak nation of Israel. If God was looking for courageous faith—gutsy warrior material—then he was peering into the wrong winepress.

But no, God wanted Gideon. When the fact finally sank in, the reluctant general began to gather a large army around him, only to find that God had different ideas. Instead of using thousands, he wanted to complete the job with a mere 300 men.

The task was ridiculously large. The enemy soldiers filled a great valley 'thick as locusts'. Their camels could no more be counted than the sand on the seashore (7:12). Yet God accomplished his plans through Gideon's little band 'in order that Israel may not boast against me that her own strength saved her'.

God will show himself mighty through weak men and women who lean hard on his strength and grace.

I started to chase this theme through the pages of my Bible. God picked David, a teenage shepherd, to slay one of the greatest fighting men this world has ever seen. He plucked elderly Sarah from the social security ranks to birth a new nation. Her gynaecologist would have laughed—everyone else did—but nine months later they were all laughing with joy over the arrival of a beautiful baby boy.

As I acknowledged my own weaknesses, I pondered these examples. It pleased God to pick the unlikely, the unlovely, the unheralded to get his job done. Now he was picking weak, ordinary me, with all my inadequacies. 'Go, mighty woman of valour...go and tell this nation and I will be with you. I am your God, I will not fail you...'

A few books later I read 1 Chronicles 18:20–21: 'Be strong and courageous and do the work. Do not be afraid or discouraged, for the Lord God, my God, is with you. He will not fail you or forsake you until all the work for the service of the temple of the Lord is finished...and every willing man skilled in any craft.'

Sure there were going to be hurdles ahead, and I would have to learn to exercise courageous faith, but the Scriptures showed me many examples of this kind of faith overcoming great obstacles. Hebrews 11, sometimes known as the Hall of Faith, contains the names of such people, including Abraham, Isaac, Jacob, Moses and Samson. They and others were recognised for their faith, even though they didn't see all of God's promises fulfilled in their lifetimes.

So began a journey through the length and breadth of New Zealand.

Although CFFD had experienced phenomenal growth during the previous year, it wasn't until the International Year of Disabled Persons that our ministry gained national prominence.

The goals of the fellowship were to bring together the church and the disabled through evangelism, encouragement, inspiration and practical service. Although our ministry focused on addressing the needs of the disabled, many people, hurting and confused by difficult circumstances, would also benefit. The launching-pad was a service at Auckland's Anglican cathedral.

A member from CFFD was asked to do a Bible reading and another a Braille reading. My own contribution was an all-too-short, eight-minute slot in a strictly timed programme. For me to deliver a message blending humour, depth and challenge all within eight minutes, with my slowness of speech, is nearly impossible. I practised for weeks until the timer on the oven clock drove me batty!

Momentum gathered as the disabled arrived at the service en masse. Our able-bodied friends and helpers quickly and efficiently seated us in our assigned area. In no time, the cathedral was crammed to capacity.

I glanced around, observing the unfamiliar scene, feeling very much like a duck out of water. Everthing appeared foreign to me—the liturgy, incense, stained glass, the ornate furniture and the clerical robes. I struggled against my ignorance, but experienced comfort through knowing God's presence.

Slowly, a young curate approached the front pews. Hesitantly he enquired as to which one of us was Margie Willers, as he wished to erect the microphone at the correct position for my chair. Having exchanged a few words, he stood aghast, obviously overcome by the enormity of my disability. He then proceeded clumsily to adjust the microphone, all the while fighting his embarrassment and anxieties.

The unfamiliar surroundings, the curate's awkward-ness and negative reaction and a vast, high society congregation made both my adrenalin and mind work overtime. How in the world would I ever come up to their level of expectation?

In the midst of all the anxiety, God's peace become my anchor as I launched into my eight-minute address. All God asks is that we give our best. He'll do the rest! And he didn't fail me.

At the conclusion, the curate's changed response as he stepped forward to disentangle the microphone was evidence that the Lord (and I) had hit the mark! 'Bravo! Bravo!' he exlaimed. 'You're amazing. My, can you communicate! I didn't think you had the ability to pull it off. You flabbergast me.'

Then, in a more serious tone, he said: 'I challenge you concerning a statement you made during your testimony: "No miracle, but a ministry." As far as I'm concerned, your ministry is a miracle!' With a 'God bless you', he abruptly turned and walked down the aisle into the vestry.

Those words deeply affected me. I recalled the hopeless prediction of the medical profession over my life as a young child: 'There's no future...put her away...forget you ever had her.' And then, my teacher, Mr Graffeti's statement: 'You're trash; rubbish that nobody knows what to do with.' Nobody knew better than I what a miracle it had proved for me to appear on that platform that evening.

The Dean's response, published in the church's bulletin the following week, echoed the curate's encouragement:

> Miss Margie Willers, a severely handicapped person, gave an address which will remain memorable in my mind. As she reflected on the plight of the disabled, she noted difficulties and challenges under which they lived.
>
> Margaret Willers surprised the congregation by stating that the most disabled person is the one who has no faith in Christ. She hammered home to us all that even in the midst of suffering her faith in Christ gave a peace and a victory over her disability. We can learn from those who suffer of God's response to their suffering, rather than asking why God should allow them to suffer. They give voice to the love of God who gives them the spiritual insight and the power to use such suffering by seeking his love and using his grace to help themselves and other people.

That year held many challenges. I still chuckle when I reflect on the speaking engagement that began with a case of mistaken identity!

The invitation, via a call from the President of Auckland's Evening Aglow Fellowship, was for me to share a short testimony at their forthcoming banquet. My heart was in my mouth. I recognised the caller—a very attractive, dignified lady of largish build, stately manner and immaculate dress—sophistication plus! We both attended the same city church, and I had been aware of a distinct awkwardness in her manner, and that she would avoid me if at all possible. So I wondered now at her enthusiasm, almost eagerness, to have me come and tell my story.

I was allowed a slot of twenty minutes. I eagerly prepared notes, wanting to give nothing but my best. I aimed high, as this was a rather highbrow occasion. The business women who had gathered were dressed in the height of elegance, superbly coiffeured, their hair and nails beautifully manicured. Great care and detail was obvious from the table adornments, fine linen, exquisite china and silverware, to the attractively decorated dishes containing a wonderful array of mouth-watering food. Beautiful floral arrangements were strategically positioned, adding colour and flair to the lushly carpeted, chanderliered room.

It was a banquet fit for a queen. I sure didn't fit the scene! If I'd worn a garment covered in diamonds it wouldn't have camouflaged the lack of co-ordination associated with my disability. Once again, I felt totally out of depth. The situation was an opportunity for me to exercise the 'courageous faith' needed to leap over walls and break down barriers.

I'll never forget the President's reaction as I was wheeled into this amazing setting. Her countenance plummeted at the shock of seeing her invited guest— me!

'Oh no, it can't be you!' she gasped, panic-stricken. 'Oh, what in the world are we going to do?' Bending down, she grabbed my hand, grasping it so tightly that her grip almost crushed my fingers. Actually, I found her reactions highly amusing. I realised she no longer wished me to be on the programme, but hadn't she been the one who had extended the invitation? The outcome of such an evening would indeed prove interesting!

Finally, forcing herself to look at me, she blurted, 'Dear, just five minutes. You'll only have five minutes. Jesus understands!'

With my speech difficulties it was impossible to present anything of lasting impact in five minutes. At that moment I made up my mind not to be intimidated. This lady had promised me twenty minutes. I'd prepared material for twenty minutes. Twenty minutes it was going to be. Already Jesus understood, and by the time I'd finished so would everyone else in the building!

Not wanting in any way to blot my copybook, I declined to take part in their sumptuous banquet, and spent the time (while they ate) praying and absorbing the scene. All too quickly dishes were cleared away, formalities conducted and I was introduced as one of the guests for that particular evening. Suddenly there I was in my chair, centre stage before my formidable audience.

'They say I have twenty minutes to educate you,' I began.

From the moment I opened my mouth the atmosphere became electric. The presence of God took over. In those twenty minutes the Holy Spirit transformed their hearts and transformed my ministry from one predominantly with disabled people to one which would be heard by wide-ranging audiences throughout the country—and even overseas.

Since then, my policy in response to invitations to speak has been to 'shoot for the stars', and if I fall back to something less, I don't mind. I hang my faith out as far as I can and try to get other disabled people to do the same. Whenever possible I involved other members from CFFD and we ministered as a team.

I often addressed different audiences two or three times a day—an exhausting schedule, especially for me. But I was buoyed along by the rewards of serving God, and pushed myself to the limit. Ministry teams composed of disabled people were completely foreign to New Zealand congregations, and we encountered mixed reactions. Many frowned and shook their heads when we first arrived. Few did so afterwards. Our message penetrated prejudices and cut people to the quick.

'I want to thank you for what you have shared tonight,' said one minister at the close of a service. 'So many young people today think a ministry is something you receive when someone lays hands on a person. I want to tell you it is not. Authority and effectiveness come through suffering, pain, trial and tribulation. Nobody ever had the anointing of the Lord without first going through God's school—and there are no shortcuts in God's school. You don't go through it in a matter of weeks or months—it can take years! But you've been through it, and that's where your ministry has derived its power from.'

He paused before continuing: 'I know much has been achieved by your coming to this church. It has been worth it to challenge the complacency of some of us who moan and groan about trivial problems. ...'

During the International Year of Disabled Persons, I felt that various churches extended invitations to us out of a sense of duty, but we rejoiced when our teams excelled beyond and above the churches' expectations. It never ceased to amaze me how God used the lives of every person on the team to minister to or challenge individual people within the various congregations and audiences.

For some it was Faye whose serene but sightless face radiated her faith as she sang of God's goodness, power and love. Others were fascinated and deeply moved by watching and listening to Bev, also blind, reading from her Braille Bible. Still others were touched by Pam, carefully lip reading as she accompanied another singer, or Ernie (disabled by polio and cancer) and Ian (a severely arthritic patient) triumphantly testifying of life in a world of pain.

We marvelled as we saw the Spirit of God touching people's lives at the most unusual times during a service. At one service in Northland, the most powerful part of the programme was the opening prayer from a man severely disabled with cerebral palsy. A friend who knew him well gave the interpretation of the words he was taking so much effort to enunciate, and the congregation was moved to tears by this man's depth of relationship with the Lord, instead perhaps of dismissing him as incapable of real thought because of his incoherent speech.

This is how one pastor recounts that service: 'Their bright faith was a tonic to the soul. So many people spend their time trying to persuade God to keep them free from life's difficulties. Here we saw people who seized difficulties by the scruff of the neck.

'To us as a congregation it seemed incredibly difficult for God-given abilities to be exercised through people with serious disabilities, especially speech impediments. But in countless ways, particularly in worship, the Spirit of the Lord came among us and touched all those present.'

'A young man whose speech had to be interpreted led us in prayer. That opening prayer ignited the whole service, leading us to the very throne of God. A sweet rendition of "In the Garden" by a lady who'd never seen dew on the roses, spoke volumes.'

'The climax was an address by a lady who wrestled to co-ordinate tongue and speech as a consequence of cerebral palsy. As she spoke, building point upon point in a well-constructed sermon that would shame many a trained preacher, we soon forgot the difficulties she wrestled with and sensed the presence of God in our midst calling us to greater effort both for the disabled and the able-bodied people in our community.'

Allow me now to introduce to you two special friends. The first is an exceptional young man named Grant Allely. Grant is severely disabled by cerebral palsy, confined to a wheelchair and dependent on others to feed, dress, bath and toilet him.

I met Grant when he was a young man in his early twenties—a shy, fearful person, almost too afraid to break from his sheltered home-life to go on an annual holiday camp for adult spastics.

Most people cannot understand Grant's speech as he struggles hard to enunciate and form words, contorting his face in the process. His words, when they emerge, often sound like nothing more than a series of exaggerated grunts, groans and guttural sounds. Communicating with Grant is not easy. However, as one perseveres and gets to know him, one learns to decipher his garbled expressions—although still having to use the utmost concentration.

Life has been far from smooth for Grant. As a youngster he suffered a great deal. Being unable to relate verbally he became the victim of much emotional and physical abuse, and even sexual harassment.

One night, in the midst of such trauma and at his wits' end, Grant experienced an amazing heavenly vision. He awoke in the dead of night and immediately felt someone's presence in the room. Gazing down to the foot of his bed he saw a figure dressed in flowing blue robes. Light emanated from this figure, illuminating the room as if it were daytime. His hair was long and brown, his face bearded. Instantly, Grant recognised him. It was Jesus.

Slowly he made his way across the room, stopping alongside Grant as he lay on his bed. Grant had the distinct impression that Jesus was choosing him, sealing him with his blessing and, in doing so, assuring him of his ongoing presence and protection.

Grant has been through many battles, but since that sacred moment he has been aware of Christ's hand on his life in a unique way. Now in his early thirties, Grant was invited to join the Agape Force. This evangelistic organisation provided outlets with new opportunities and horizons—in fact, a whole new world, for him. Within a short time he became involved with the others, street witnessing among the evening shoppers that crowded in and out of Queen Street on Friday nights.

Grant, a twinkle in his eye, recalled: 'I'll never forget this young guy, all eager and enthusiastic to show me the action.' He chortled. 'The street was crowded.

Time seemed to tick by. I became aware that I'd been wheeled through the same shopping mall for the umpteenth time at a fast pace yet going nowhere! Suddenly it dawned on me—the young man wheeling me had got stage fright. The truth was, he felt out of his depth coping with me, let alone tackling street witnessing!'

The young man may have copped out, but Grant was determined not to allow this grand opportunity to slip by. The greatest thing in life, for Grant, was to see people committing their lives to Jesus Christ. With his new friend freaked-out, there wasn't anyone else around to be his mouthpiece, so Grant himself took the plunge. He stepped out in faith, trusting God to do the supernatural.

What happened next can only be described as a miracle. Grant suddenly felt supercharged by the Spirit of God. With reasonable clarity of speech he began sharing the gospel, and saw it having a pro-found effect on several who stopped to listen—an amazing experience for both Grant and his tongue-tied companion.

Grant's employment prospects are nil. Before the introduction of Agape Force, most of his days had been spent within the confinement of his home, but then he thought about the many hours he dwindled away each day and came to the realisation that every day was a gift from God. In a matter of days, Grant was courageously venturing out in his chair, awkwardly using his foot to kick himself backwards down the pavement to the shops at the end of his street. Across the front of his wheelchair he'd attached a tray which displayed an assortment of little books and tracts. His brother had produced a sign and attached this to Grant's tray. It read: 'You may not understand my speech, but please let me share Jesus with you! Help yourself to one of my books—they are free!'

At first, many ignored him but Grant persisted in his

new venture—and God honoured his tenacity. It wasn't long before people did stop to speak with Grant and took time to read a little booklet or one of his tracts. Later some of them told how the courageous faith of this young man made a profound spiritual impact on their lives.

Despite the enormity of his disability, Grant has persevered and accomplished many good things for God. One of these includes Radio Rhema, a Christian radio station which broadcasts from a network of stations in New Zealand. Because he was confined indoors a great deal, Radio Rhema became Grant's special companion throughout the day. He longed for other disabled people to enjoy such stimulating Christian programmes.

Rhema had applied again and again for a permanent Auckland licence, but each time permission was refused. While most Christians accepted the decision, Grant would not sit back and take 'no' for an answer. So he determined to do something positive about procuring a licence.

He organised a petition to Parliament and sent copies to those whom he thought would support the venture throughout the North Island.

The results were disappointing. Two weeks prior to the petition's closure, few had been returned, and of those that had, some only listed three or four signatures. But Grant wasn't about to be beaten. He insisted that a friend take him, along with his petition, to the Easter Show where he spent many hours gaining support for Rhema from the thousands who thronged the gates.

On other days, regardless of the weather, he'd propel himself to a large supermarket nearby and invite shoppers to give their support. Through these efforts alone he obtained 61,000 signatures. The local Member of Parliament was so impressed with Grant's zeal that he took the petition down to Wellington where it was read out in New Zealand's House of Representatives.

CFFD quickly recognised the part Grant could play in its activities and church services. He was encouraged to write short sermons, which he typed out to be read by a friend. These deeply challenging messages may have been read in a few minutes, but it often took Grant up to four or five hours of labour at the keyboard of his electronic typewriter to compile his material.

For some time Grant and I both attended the same church, and we were usually positioned alongside each other. Hugh and Di would sit nearby to assist us with things like the offering bags and communion cups.

One Sunday morning service, while I was meditatively drinking my communion wine, my thoughts were jolted by a loud echoing crunch beside me. Worriedly I glanced over, and to my amazement and mirth I watched Hugh determinedly trying to control himself as he extracted the remains of the communion cup from Grant's mouth. Cautiously he fished around with his fingers, attempting to pick out all the pieces. Grant's front tooth had become caught in the cup's rim and his automatic reaction was to clench his teeth, crunching the thing into a dozen pieces. Hugh did his best, but amid the splutters and snorts of convulsive laughter, Grant proceeded to spit out bits of white plastic. People turned in their pews, distracted and alarmed by the apparent deliverance session! (Understandably there are moments when the two of us are together that our friends and family would rather not admit knowing us!)

Taking an active part within CFFD team ministry to the churches built up Grant's self-esteem, giving him purpose in life. Gradually, this uncomplaining but rather passive young man who had conditioned himself to allowing everything to be done for him, had developed surprising initiative and enterprise.

It was Eddie Cairns who was quick to sense Grant's special abilities. Eddie is director of Mission Outreach —an organisation which regularly smuggles Bibles into communist countries. He encouraged Grant to see the vital role he could play in praying for imprisoned Christians. After all, Grant could readily identify with those suffering behind the Iron Curtain, for wasn't he also in prison within the confines of his wheelchair?

Grant was astonished to think that he too could contribute something powerful to this dangerous yet exciting ministry. But prayer wasn't where it stopped! Grant never tired of listening to the thrilling accounts by Brother Andrew and others who had returned from taking Bibles into China. How he'd love to experience this adventure! As he pondered and prayed about it, the idea that he too could be involved became less and less preposterous.

Stepping out in faith, he enquired about the air fare to China—$NZ2,500. Grant knew that if God was in this dream then he would provide, somehow. He also knew that God doesn't help those who don't help themselves, so he made a start towards raising his air fare. He earned his first $20 through typing. The twenty pages involved five days of intense concentration as he pecked his way through the task using the head-wand fixed to a specially designed helmet. Then CFFD accepted one of his computer drawings for its 1987 Christmas card production. This sparked a further idea. Why not produce a variety of designs and cards of his own?

Back to the computer he went where he planned the layout, designed a selection of scenes and produced accompanying inscriptions. He then photocopied 1,200 cards. These all sold. At 15c each, they provided another $180. This, along with his initial $20, equalled $200. $2,300 to go!

I believe God's heart was touched by such courageous faith, as were the hearts of others. The small church fellowship which Grant now attended threw a surprise birthday party. Gifts were in the form of cheques, mounting to another $NZ700 for his 'Mission Impossible.'

In the next month God opened the windows of heaven and poured down financial blessing. Grant could hardly contain his excitement, for God had provided his complete fare, plus spending money!

At last the day arrived when we bid farewell to a very excited Grant along with his two travelling companions. Days later the triumphant news came— 'Mission fulfilled!' Grant had hidden his large consignment of Bibles in his wheelchair bag, then agonised as a Chinese soldier paced back and forth while he waited and waited and waited in the designated place for his delayed contact. Just how the delivery was transacted remains a secret, but what a memorable day we experienced as we welcomed back our jubilant smuggler!

Grant continues to be an inspiration to all who come in contact with him, proving that with God it's not our ability that counts but our availability.

The second friend I'd like to introduce you to is Margaret Thomson. Margaret also suffers from cerebral palsy, and sometimes uses a wheelchair, although she can propel her body along with the aid of crutches.

Like Grant, Margaret also has a severe speech impediment and she communicates mainly by punching out sentences on a Canon communicator. Margaret is a highly intelligent lady, a graduate from the Bible College of New Zealand. For an able-bodied student this course would normally involve two to three years' study, but it took Margaret four years' long haul before she graduated.

Towards the end of the final semester she was honoured by a request from the college faculty to address the entire student body. Margaret worked hard, labouring long hours on her message before the day arrived when a friend with a clear strong voice read her address for her.

Margaret sat slumped in her wheelchair on the platform. Sometimes her arms jerked uncontrollably, and her head sagged down so it touched her shoulders. Occasionally saliva dribbled from her mouth. Margaret had chosen as her text: 'We have this treasure in earthen vessels.'

Students who had once avoided Margaret now saw her, for the first time, as a whole person. They heard profound and beautiful words as they looked on the tragic human figure.

For me, this is an illustration of the church. Christ is the Head and for the body he has a bunch of spastics like us. Glimpse for a moment the humiliation of that. God on high exalting us in allowing us to be carriers of his living Spirit.

Without a doubt, the biggest thrill of my life is seeing people, able and disabled, allowing Jesus Christ into their lives and opening themselves to his freeing power, becoming all they were created for. Hundreds of people were touched and challenged through CFFD's ministry to the churches.

All credit for my own ministry must go to God. Only he could take my voice and make my speech intelligible. Sometimes I experienced surges of heat flowing through my body when I preached. At other times, I felt nothing. Often, the anointing rested on my hearers. God is a God of variety—he moves in mysterious ways, performing his wonders.

There were times when I felt more than a little jaded, and on one such occasion I am convinced that God sent an angel in disguise to encourage my flagging spirits. It was in the form of a handsome, blond-haired man who crouched beside my chair. Striving to compose himself, he began to tell me his story.

'Margie, you won't remember me, but I just want to

encourage you in your ministry. I will never forget the day you addressed our chapel members. I was a hard man then, bitter and twisted. There was no love in my home. My wife hated me and the children feared me and showed me no respect. While I listened as you recounted your story, God brought about a miracle.

'The dam of hatred and bitterness I'd held within me for years burst in a flood of tears. I fell on my knees and cried to the Lord, begging forgiveness. The commitment was a body, soul, mind and heart commitment. I realised God wasn't interested in anything less!

'I wanted to talk with you that day, but I was too broken, too emotionally washed up to do so. But I'm telling you now. God has transformed my marriage— my wife loves me and my children no longer fear me; they now have a healthy love and respect for me as their dad.'

Then he choked out nine devastating words: 'Thank you, Margie, for not being healed in America!'

By the time he had finished, I was crying. I bowed my head as I acknowledged God's wisdom in not healing me.

As the meeting got under way, I noticed a young man causing a considerable disturbance at the back of the church. Finally, he stomped out of the building. Apparently, I'd lit his fuse. My message had triggered something deep within and he was furious. His story was told to me a few days later. His mother had been confined to a wheelchair for almost five years with multiple sclerosis. His father had deserted the family, and shortly afterwards the three eldest children had also walked out, leaving him with the responsibility of caring for an ailing mother. The burden imposed tremendous demands on one so young, and he struggled with a sense of injustice, disillusionment and hurt.

If faced with the same circumstances we too might

be tempted to throw the question in God's face—
'Where's your fairness when disability won't go away?'

Walking out of the service, he had tramped the
streets for miles, remonstrating with God into the early
hours of the morning.

Finally, having poured out all his vehemence, he
knelt under a street lamp and invited Jesus Christ into
his life—and his mother's gruelling situation. The
anger he had harboured against God for five years,
and the rebellious spirit that had become a driving
force in him relaxed their grip as Christ took control.
Some months lapsed. Little by little, God replaced this
young man's insolence and anger with his love and his
compassion. The promise of 2 Corinthians 5:17 is that
a person in Christ becomes a new creature. Old habits
and attitudes are replaced as the Spirit of God works in
a person's life. Today, I know of no more precious
relationship between mother and son than that shown
by those two.

One of the greatest barriers I face in ministry is
negative attitudes. Because of the enormity of my
disability and my slowness of speech, people naturally
jump to conclusions that my brain must be the same!

I well remember a women's meeting in Northland.
As Di wheeled me into the building we were immediately conscious of shocked reactions from the
audience as they realised the guest speaker was
wheelchair-bound.

Di calmly positioned my chair close to the microphone. We exchanged knowing glances before surveying an audience of bewildered faces. I struggled to
maintain a right attitude, for this proved to be the most
daunting congregation I'd ever faced. To cap it all, a
pastor slowly sidled alongside my chair, hesitating
before producing a hymn book. Placing it on my lap,
he started to ask me to choose an appropriate number
for the altar call. Then, as if I were deaf, he loudly
hissed to Di: 'Er, excuse me, but can this woman read?'

I trust this man pardoned my rudeness as I let out my loudest snort. How in the world did he expect me to preach if I couldn't read?

That day I chose to exercise 'courageous faith' and claimed God's promise that he would be with me. Forcing aside my own misgivings and the congregation's obvious prejudice, I launched into a thought-provoking message entitled 'God's fairness when disability won't go away'. Never have I preached with such fervency. God made his presence felt as his spirit moved along row after row, individual after individual. Jesus walked the aisles touching lives and changing hearts. People laughed. People cried. People broke into spontaneous applause. But, most important, people encountered the reality of a living God.

God taught me a valuable lesson that day. Yes, I was bound in a wheelchair—but in body only!

As the year continued unfolding, my itinerary gathered momentum, climaxing in a fourteen-day journey to three of New Zealand's major centres: Wellington, Christchurch and Dunedin. This schedule would have proved demanding for any person, as there were often two or three speaking engagements per day. For me, it was a monumental undertaking. Often after being carried off stage I would sleep like the dead for an hour or two before being revived to fulfil the next engagement. Christ's strength was certainly made perfect in my weakness. His divine enabling allowed me to enjoy blessing upon blessing throughout the entire tour.

Most memorable was the afternoon I was invited to speak at a large camp at Living Springs Convention Centre, a magnificent ranch-type building nestled between the mountain ranges south of Christchurch. My audience consisted of about 400 young people in the fifteen to thirty age group. Accompanying me, as part of the programme, were other disabled people

from the Christchurch CFFD branch who had con-
tributed with drama, testimony and song prior to my
address. It went well. The young people responded
enthusiastically.

At the conclusion, the camp chairman, a prominent
minister in the area, stood behind the pulpit and made
a public confession: 'Margie, I was told you were
disabled, therefore I prepared myself to meet someone
in a wheelchair, but not someone with imperfect
speech. I confess to being prejudiced by your outward
appearance and praying, "Lord, I sure don't want her
on this platform—she can't even speak properly,
nobody will understand a word!" I made my judge-
ments even before I'd heard your testimony or seen
you in action.'

Tears spilled down his face. 'Forgive me, please, for
having the audacity to think it's education and ability
that count. I heard you issue your challenge and I saw
people rock in their pews. In all my life, never have I
been so challenged...Through you, God has taught
me never to judge a person by what they appear to be.
In the hands of God your potential is limitless. Truly,
you are "a mighty woman of valour".'

A few days later a telephone call came for me from a
television producer inviting me to share on overcoming disability and the work of the Christian
Fellowship for Disabled. My heart was in my mouth
as my host stood by the phone writing down the information. We agreed to an interview in three days' time. I'm
no TV star, and I expressed real reservations about
appearing on such a programme. What about my facial
contortions? Slowness of speech? Awkward, involuntary movements? But all my objections were ignored.

The big day arrived. I met the television director
who explained procedures to me and discussed
possible interview questions, making me feel more
relaxed and comfortable. After a visit from the television's make-up lady, I found myself seated opposite

Jim Mora in the studio. Lights flooded the set with warmth and brightness. Mora smiled and glanced quickly at his notes. 'Just relax,' he encouraged.

'Fifteen seconds!' someone called from behind the cameras. I wasn't as tense or nervous as I thought I might be—probably because I knew what I planned to say, and was glad that my testimony and the ministry of the Christian Fellowship for Disabled would be shared with many thousands of people. I didn't know for sure what Jim Mora planned to ask me, but I knew of nothing he could ask that would make me uncomfortable.

'Ten seconds!'

'Lord,' I prayed, 'give me confidence, clarity of speech, wisdom, body control and the opportunity to make all this meaningful.'

'Five seconds!'

I swallowed and wet my lips, watching the floor director count down with his fingers: 'Three, two, one.'

A red light on top of the camera went on and Jim Mora turned towards it. 'We have in the studio Miss Margie Willers, Founding President of the Christian Fellowship for Disabled here in New Zealand. The fellowship caters for all disabilities and provides a network of branches which specialise in meeting the social, physical and other needs of the disabled. Margie herself is disabled by cerebral palsy and has a unique story to tell.'

I don't recall all I said, except that our conversation was natural. His questions enabled me to share important parts of my testimony and, although time was limited, I was still able to give good input on the work of the fellowship. In fact, I was able to say everything I wanted to say.

As the production crew began putting things away, turning off the lights and placing lens caps on cameras, I finally had time to reflect on what had happened.

'Just think,' remarked my friend who'd been assigned

as my helper for that day, 'you probably talked to a million people today about your faith! That's quite an opportunity.'

Many people who watched the TV programme either telephoned or wrote expressing positive comments about what I had said. Some wanted further information about the work of the fellowship. Others enquired about my availability to speak in their churches. Still others asked questions about my experiences. I could see the Lord was going to use this TV interview to broaden my scope of witness still further and open many more doors—doors leading on to university campuses, medical schools, Rotary meetings and Bible colleges.

On my arrival back home in Auckland, I received a letter from Jim Mora.

'All of us are horrified when seeing or hearing ourselves through the electronic media for the first time,' he wrote. 'In your case, I honestly feel you have reason to be proud of your communicatory ability. Lord knows, I've met a pretty wide cross-section of people in my career, but your interview will remain in my mind long after I've forgotten nearly all the others. I envy your faith. It gives you a strength that most of us don't possess, despite our outward appearances.'

In this old wheelchair, God has taken me from the tip of New Zealand to its toe. I've shared my story with the uttermost and the guttermost, to the captive and the free. But the most indelible experience occurred when I was invited to share with the inmates of Auckland's Maximum Security Prison.

I had heard frightening stories about this massive place, housing hundreds of inmates who had committed every conceivable crime. It was a scorching hot summer's day and I'd been invited to share in the chapel service in the prison's common room.

My tension and nervousness mounted as killers, robbers, rapists, drug pushers and violent criminals entered the room. The inmates were lavishly tattooed —some had '666' engraved on their foreheads; others had rings in their ears and noses. Some appeared to be high on dope, and many of them were unwashed and unkempt. There wasn't a 'normal' person in sight! The big attraction drawing inmates to the chapel service was the entertainment value and anticipation of female company.

About 145 inmates ambled in, surveying the scene. Obviously the entertainment wasn't up to their expectation, and neither was my sex appeal, because within minutes forty to fifty disgruntled, mumbling inmates sauntered back out again.

As I spoke, many began to mimick me and jeer while others did perfect imitations of cerebral palsy. I went hot and cold, wondering how in the world I would relate to this lot! Feeling extremely vulnerable, I frantically prayed, searching for the right introduction to begin my testimony.

Taking a deep breath, I began by describing my body as a prison, I'd hardly uttered the words when the Spirit of God filled the building. I spoke for twenty-five minutes or so on the challenges of overcoming in God...Faith Bible College...the Rider on the white horse...the call to ministry.

I have seen many congregations moved to tears, but to see tough, hardened criminals blubbering almost made me cry too.

Ten minutes into my story three inmates started a disturbance. Instantly a huge guy, seated on the opposite side of the hall, rose to his feet. Stalking across, he confronted the trouble-makers, giving all three a swift kick in the shins. Then he ordered, 'Shut your faces and listen, you hear me? She's worth it!'

The hair stood up on the back of my neck. I could almost visualise headlines in the daily newspaper— 'Woman in wheelchair causes riot!' To my amazement, they sat transfixed, unable to move.

Another young inmate eyed me defiantly, determined I'd never relate to him nor his situation. In the natural that was very true, but having God on my side, he'd met his match! Halfway through my talk he fell forward in his chair, dropped his head in his hands and his tears splashed onto the floor. When I'd finished he sat up, grinned at me through his tears and then joined in the applause.

As the church members responsible for prison ministry interacted with the inmates I too mixed freely, speaking with the various prisoners. While doing so I met a Christian inmate. He hugged me. On enquiring how long he'd been living in the institute, he calmly replied, 'I'm serving a life sentence.' I tried hard not to balk. This was my first close encounter with a killer!

'Margie,' he said, 'You'll never know how much you've helped me today. What courageous faith you possess! What an encouragement! Pardon me, but in heaven, when you dance in your yellow dress, white shoes and pearl necklace, may I have the first dance?'

Epilogue

I had been speaking at a church one evening. The meeting had come to an end and people were milling around my chair. Suddenly a woman brushed through the crowd and thrust an ugly, dark object into my hand. At first glance it appeared to be a dried prune.

The woman eyed me squarely, then briskly stated: 'This, to me,' is a perfect illustration of your life's worth and that of your ministry. Please keep it as a reminder—use it whenever possible. I want you to keep it, it's yours!' Then she was gone.

Who was this woman? I wondered. Was she a lunatic, or was she being downright cruel?

Moments ticked by before I plucked up the courage to examine the dark object more closely. Instantly tears smarted my eyes. I realised that I'd greatly misjudged this lady for she'd paid me a most beautiful compliment. On closer observation, I found the object to be a little rock, split in two. Although outwardly ugly, inside it had a beautiful silver core. Immediately I understood her point. My bodily appearance was unattractive and unappealing, but it's not the externals of life that count with God, it's the beauty of character radiating from within. I still treasure that little rock and the illustration it portrays.

The vision of myself dancing in my yellow dress, wearing white shoes and a pearl necklace has long since died. Although my vision failed, the call to the highways and byways is being fulfilled.

As I was lifted onto the platform to deliver my final address in conjunction with the International Year of Disabled Persons, the programme bearers casually commented: 'Margie, God has taken this chair and used your remarkable story to turn pain to pearls in the lives of thousands throughout this nation.'

Again tears of gratitude smarted my eyes. I reflected on the prophetic words of the usher who'd prayed with me for those five hours at Kathryn Kuhlman's miracle service. 'God has chosen you and called you to speak to crowds of people—and to be his witness before large congregations. . . .' Having proclaimed 'the word of the Lord', he had disputed that the prophecy could ever be fulfilled from my wheelchair. But God is the God of the impossible, and he is not limited by disability.

Once I hankered for a physical miracle but, as yet, this miracle has not come about. Instead, there has been a ministry, which in itself is a miracle!

Many things in life have been denied me. The possibility of being a wife is fairly remote, and I will never experience normal childbirth. Instead God has given to me the role of spiritual motherhood, and in this I find endless encouragement. I take heart in Isaiah 54:1, 'Sing, O barren woman. . .burst into song, shout for joy you who were never in labour; because more are the children of the desolate woman than of her who has a husband.'

For me, Christian ministry has become an on-going adventure. I started within the relatively narrow confines of the disabled world, moved on to the able-bodied world and now teach regularly in Bible colleges throughout New Zealand. My wheelchair has pushed open doors and pushed down barriers—just as Sister Joy prophesied. I try to help Christian leaders and potential leaders to see the need for balance and sensitivity regarding suffering and the sovereignty of

God. So often seemingly mature Christians say to me, 'When I see you rise and walk from your chair, then I will really worship God.' Such triumphalistic attitudes sadden me, and must grieve God. No wonder revival is not sweeping our land when people are waiting for God to prove himself. God does not have to prove himself—with the spectacular or any other means. God is God. He is sovereign.

So often we only worship him when he lives up to our expectations. I still grapple with many issues regarding healing and non-healing. I certainly don't have all the answers, and I have real reservations about those who claim they do. But one thing I have learned is that God deals with us as individuals. What he does for one person he may not do for the next. He may heal one, while another remains in a wheelchair. Why he works that way, I do not know. Nor do I know why some have so much pain, sorrow and tears in their lives while others don't.

In the modern world where everything is instant and very few people are prepared to wait for anything, we often want to skip the difficult times of life. But without a certain tension in our lives, and without a willingness to live by faith without all the answers, God cannot work as deeply as he could in our lives.

The apostle Paul wrote that God's revelation to him was so tremendous that in order to prevent him from becoming conceited he was given a 'thorn of flesh'. Whether it was physical or spiritual is irrelevent. The point is he had a problem and it bugged him. Three times he begged the Lord for the thorn to be removed, but God gave a definite 'no'. And that was that. True Christian maturity involves accepting God's 'no' and facing up to the fact that we simply don't have all the answers. Paul rejoiced—he had a positive attitude.

Sometimes God removes a circumstance by his power, and sometimes he takes a person through a circumstance by his power. The reason he takes you through it is to make you strong. The same power that took Daniel through the lion's den also gave Stephen strength as he was stoned to death.

'Father,' he prayed.

That was supernatural. That was not human. To be human is to shake your fist into the face of those who are attacking you. Only supernatural love gives you the power to love your enemies. That love is the power of God. The power that healed the lame man at the gate of the temple in Acts Chapter Four was the same power that gave Paul the strength to endure his thorn in the flesh. The same power that sent an angel to release Peter from prison also enabled Paul to remain in prison to die. The same power that took Jesus through the Garden of Gethsemane also raised him three days later.

All the great concepts of Scripture would fall in a pile on the floor if, at the flick of a switch, God's power made things happen automatically every time we went to him. If we were never tested and tried we would never mature. For me, faith isn't getting what I want—it's getting what God wants. I can now say from experience that I would rather live in a wheelchair and have a deep relationship with Jesus Christ than stand on two feet and not know him at all.

Consider the story of Shadrach, Meshach and Abednego—three men of tremendous faith who were willing to trust God despite the cost. They refused to bow to a heathen god, instead choosing a fiery death in King Nebuchadnezzar's furnace. But the furnace held no fears for Shadrach, Meshach and Abednego. They told the king that even if they were thrown into the fire, their God was able to deliver them from it. But even if he did not deliver them, they still wouldn't bow down to the heathen god.

What is your fiery furnace? Is it working through a lost love, divorce, death of a loved one, a financial crisis? Or is it life in a wheelchair? God did not prevent the three men being thrown into the fire. Instead he went into the fire with them. I'd rather know the power and presence of God in my circumstances. God's perspective is very different from ours. As the Bible says, 'For my thoughts are not your thoughts, neither are your ways my ways' (Isa 55:8).

God can and does heal supernaturally, but sometimes he chooses not to heal. For me, faith is living for God and trusting him when I don't have all the answers.